Business
Plan

Other books about running a small business from How To Books

85 INSPIRING WAYS TO MARKET YOUR SMALL BUSINESS
Inspiring, self-help, sales and marketing strategies that you can apply to
your own business immediately
JACKIE JARVIS

THE SMALL BUSINESS START-UP WORKBOOK
A step-by-step guide to starting the business you've dreamed of
CHERYL D RICKMAN

PREPARE TO SELL YOUR COMPANY
A guide to planning and implementing a successful exit
L B BUCKINGHAM

BOOK-KEEPING AND ACCOUNTING FOR THE SMALL BUSINESS
How to keep the accounts and maintain financial control over your business
PETER TAYLOR

SETTING UP AND RUNNING A LIMITED COMPANY
A comprehensive guide to forming and operating a company as a director
and shareholder
ROBERT BROWNING

Write or phone for a catalogue to:

How To Books
Spring Hill House
Spring Hill Road
Begbroke
Oxford
OX5 1RX
Tel. 01865 375794

Or email: info@howtobooks.co.uk

Visit our website www.howtobooks.co.uk to find out more about us and our books.

Like our Facebook page **How To Books & Spring Hill**

Follow us on **Twitter @Howtobooksltd**

Read our books online www.howto.co.uk

Write Your Own
Business
Plan

Build a plan that will secure finance
and transform your business

PAUL HETHERINGTON

howtobooks

Published by How To Books Ltd,
Spring Hill House, Spring Hill Road,
Begbroke, Oxford OX5 1RX
Tel: (01865) 375794. Fax: (01865) 379162
info@howtobooks.co.uk
www.howtobooks.co.uk

How To Books greatly reduce the carbon footprint of their books by sourcing their typesetting and printing in the UK.

British Library Cataloguing in Publication Data
A catalogue record for this book is available from the British Library

ISBN: 978 1 84528 486 2

Produced for How To Books by Deer Park Productions, Tavistock
Typeset by TW Typesetting, Plymouth, Devon
Printed and bound in Great Britain by Bell & Bain Ltd, Glasgow

NOTE: The material contained in this book is set out in good faith for general guidance and no liability can be accepted for loss or expense incurred as a result of relying in particular circumstances on statements made in the book. The laws and regulations are complex and liable to change, and readers should check the current position with the relevant authorities before making personal arrangements.

MIX
Paper from
responsible sources
FSC
www.fsc.org
FSC® C007785

To my wife and best friend, Susan Margaret

CONTENTS

List of figures

List of tables

Preface

Everyone who manages a business spends time planning. Virtually everybody wants to improve their business in some way or other and without planning it is unlikely to happen. How the planning is done varies widely. For many people the whole thing is very informal and unstructured. Planning may simply consist of lone musing or endless discussions with a partner while trying to decide what needs to be done differently. Often, very little is actually written down – maybe just a few notes of what needs to be done. It isn't really a very efficient use of planning time but many people seem to get by on it.

What happens when you decide that you need to borrow money? You will probably meet your bank manager or some other funder and soon get asked for a copy of your business plan. A few scribbled notes on the back of an envelope will no longer suffice.

WHY THE FUNDER WANTS TO SEE A PLAN

The main concern of funders is that they will get their money back. The most likely way for that to happen is through the success of the business. From experience, funders know that businesses with well researched, clearly laid-out plans are more likely to be successful than businesses without. So you need a plan to convince the funder that the project will work and the investment will be repaid.

Viewers of the popular TV series *Dragon's Den* will have seen at first hand how investors think. Most of the questions asked by the dragons refer to the business plan for the project. They try to determine how well the project has been researched, whether the team have the skills necessary for its success and whether the numbers add up. So you will need to understand your plan well enough to answer any questions confidently and the best way to do that is to research and write it yourself.

WHAT ELSE CAN A PLAN DO?

Many people think that, when the funding has been achieved, the plan has done its job. They put the plan on the shelf, then simply forget about it and get on with running the business.

If you do that you miss out on what is probably the best aid to successfully running a business there is. It will provide a guideline on what to do after you receive the investment to give yourself the best possible chance of being spectacularly successful. Spectacular success is unlikely to come to those who haven't planned for it. It doesn't come overnight either. This book will show you how to create realistic business objectives and cascade them down to personal objectives, so individuals know what they have to do.

Objectives should not be set in stone. Fortune telling has no place in planning: you never know what the future holds. Be prepared to review your results regularly and adapt objectives where necessary. Great leaders are great improvisers, but they always have a good plan to start with.

So the prime purpose of your plan should be to help you achieve your dreams; to help you take your business to where you really want it to be. Somewhat ironically, plans that have been written specifically to help owners achieve the results they desire are more likely to achieve funding successfully than those written simply to raise investment. The funder's first concern is that the project will be successful. A plan which is clearly set out to achieve the desired results and form a blueprint for running the business will be more likely to satisfy the funder.

HOW TO USE THIS BOOK

This book is set out in the order you should use to prepare and write your business plan rather than the layout of the plan itself. When creating your plan, some things need to be completed before others can be started, whereas your reader wants everything presented as a logical story of your business. For example, your readers will want the plan to start with an executive summary so that they can get a quick overall picture, but you cannot write this until last.

You may, however, not have the time to work through the step-by-step process of formulating a brilliant plan, but need a plan very quickly. Chapter 3 contains a sample business plan which is intended as an example of what the final thing may look like. In desperate circumstances it could be used as the basis of a quick plan, but this is not an approach I would recommend. It is still vital that you get your numbers right. Make sure you read Chapter 16 carefully. An alternative method for a quick and dirty plan is to use business plan software that asks you to fill in the gaps, but the approach is again not recommended. It leads towards a paper plan without due consideration of strategy.

The book has been designed as a management development tool. Most sections have been written at three levels to make them appropriate to teams at all stages of their development. *Level 1* is aimed at people who have no experience of business planning and is the minimum needed to produce a professional plan. *Level 3* is for experienced planners and is intended to guide them into writing a plan equivalent to that they would get by having a professional to do it for them. Having researched and written it themselves, however, will mean they both better understand it and more strongly identify with it. Resultantly this should facilitate its use as an ongoing business aid rather than something which looks pretty but sits on the shelf. *Level 2* is our suggested intermediary path between the two extremes.

However, it is your business and your plan. You choose at what level you wish to work for each section, depending on your business and your team's experience. The whole concept is completely mix and match, so you can get a plan which is right for your stage of development. Used properly, business planning is one of the best business development tools there is. Year by year your team will grow in experience and confidence as they take your plan up through the levels, expanding your goals and working towards achieving them.

As the planning skills of your team develop, you will possibly find that you are at level 1 in some aspects, and level 2 or level 3 in others. Teams develop fastest in the areas in which they have the most expertise. As an example, a team of accountants would probably start at level 3 in the financial aspects and possibly level 1 in the marketing part. Conversely, a sophisticated marketing team may start at level 3 in the marketing part of the plan and Level 1 in finance.

One word of warning: do not try to push yourself too fast. It is better to plan well at a lower level than to take on too much. You should try to up your game year by year, but this is better done in measured steps.

Working at your comfort level in each part of the plan is vital. This book is designed to be the essential reference point for teams at all the different levels of sophistication in their approach to management. It is suitable for the full range: from blue-chip corporations that want to become stronger to micro-businesses with big ideas.

Each chapter contains worksheets to help you gather and analyse information. There is also a business plan builder for each level to help you gather together what you have discovered. When working at level 2 or 3, the material covered in the lower level(s) will generally be used, but only use the business plan builder of the level you are working at unless instructed otherwise. When you write the relevant part of the plan, don't just copy the contents of the business plan builder and worksheets in, but try to make a story out of it. If some of the information doesn't look very relevant there is no need to include it.

The principal aim of this book is to help you crystallise your dreams for the business and produce a plan that will help you achieve the results you want. This approach will also help you raise the necessary finance.

If you have any questions, catch up with the blog: http://www.phct.co.uk/blog/. Templates are available at the website.

1

Deciding what your business plan is for

You have probably picked up this book because someone has asked you for a business plan. On the other hand, you may have heard that businesses with formally written plans generally make a lot more profit than ones without.

Whatever your main reason for writing a plan is, you will probably find that there are secondary uses you want to put it to. In each case it is essential that you first clarify what exactly the purpose is and who the reader is going to be. Different readers have different priorities and will focus on different aspects of the plan. Just to produce one plan and then simply give a copy to whomever needs it will probably be unsuccessful. A better idea is to produce a version of the plan aimed specifically at the reader who needs it. We are not talking about different plans, but essentially different versions of the same basic plan.

Each plan must still be a true representation of your business. They will all be basically the same plan, but tweaked to give them a different focus; whatever will make it most likely to bring about the desired response from that reader.

EXTERNAL PLANS

These are produced for readers who are external to the business. They would generally include the main business objectives but not the detailed tactical plans that are essential to successful implementation. Too much detail would probably bog the plan down in the eyes of a professional but you still need to be able to answer any questions about its implementation.

There is always the risk that a plan will get into the hands of a competitor. Don't give away business secrets or include sensitive information. Funders will generally ask for specific information they need. On the other hand, don't get paranoid and hold back information that should be included. That can result in rejection out of hand.

INTERNAL PLANS

These are produced for various people inside the business. They are commonly used to communicate to the workforce what the organisation is planning to do, having more emphasis on how the plans will be implemented and less on sensitive information which the workforce is not privy to.

In a larger organisation they are often used as an aid to securing the budget a unit needs, and to obtain approval for what the management seeks to do.

WHAT PLANS ARE COMMONLY USED FOR

Potential investor

This is commonly a business angel, a venture capitalist or maybe someone you know who is interested in investing in your business. The business plan is generally the most important document on which they will base their decision. Essential supplementary documents such as trading accounts tend simply to support the business plan.

Table 1.1   Common uses of plans

Reader	Goal	Main focus	Key performance indicator
Potential investor	Share purchase	High return	Growth
Bank manager	Loan approval	Security	Cash flow
Business purchaser	Sell the business	Structure	Net profit
Potential partner	Joint venture	Resource	Operations
Tender assessor	Win tender	Capability	Turnover
Grant fund-holder	Win grant	Social	Strategy
Team	Direction	Communication	Various

Potential investors understand that they are making a fairly high-risk investment and as compensation are looking for the opportunity of receiving high gains. An angel or venture capitalist will typically be looking for a 60% return on capital per annum. They often look at an investment horizon of something like 5 years. A return of 60% a year over five years will give an investor ten times the sum invested. If as an example £100,000 was invested they would expect to get £1 million after five years. They would not generally expect to get any dividends during the five years as profits would probably be reinvested to maintain high growth.

To satisfy a professional investor the plan would have to explain a plausible strategy for achieving the necessary growth rate. If as the owner you do not want to pursue a high-growth strategy, seeking investment from angels or venture capitalists may not be the right option for you.

Venture capitalists are organisations that tend to focus on the larger (multi-million pound) investments, while angels are usually high net worth individuals who are usually looking at smaller investments, generally in the range of £20,000–£200,000. They tend to have particular areas of interest. When you look at a list of investors, pay particular attention to the type of project they specialise in and their target amount of investment. Only approach the ones who seem interested in what you do.

As their main interest is growth, you will need to focus your plan on that, especially the executive summary. Ensure your strategy backs up this expectation of high growth with strong market analysis. You will also need to demonstrate how you plan to build capacity and resources to support the growth in sales.

Investors expect shares in the business and this dilutes the ownership.

Bank manager

More plans are probably written for the bank than anything else. Most businesses need the support of their bankers in some way or other. Whether it's simply an overdraft facility that is needed to aid cash flow, or a fixed-period loan is required to fund capital expenditure, bank managers will generally respond in the same way. They will want to see a business plan before approving the application.

Bank managers only have one real concern. That is getting their money back. They want a low-risk investment. They are always looking for security so that, if the business fails, they can still get their money back through the security. If the business is a limited company they will try to get the directors to make personal guarantees on the borrowed amount. When the directors sign those guarantees they essentially lose the benefit of limited liability, as the debt will become theirs in the event of business failure.

Bank managers prefer to see steady growth rather than high growth, as that carries less risk. They like to see a business built on solid foundations, with evidence of good management and steady profits. The cash-flow forecast is very important to them as it will indicate the funding requirement of the business. You will need to demonstrate exactly how that funding require-ment will be met. It may well be a combination of loans and investment from directors, a fixed-term bank loan and an overdraft.

A plan for a bank manager needs to emphasise the solidarity of the business and the low risk of the investment. It probably needs to be fairly conservative. You should be confident that the targets in it will be met. It is very easy to lose the support of your friendly bank manager in subsequent years if a plan was seen to have been over-ambitious. If you've done better than forecasted, fine, but if you have failed to reach your targets you will then be regarded with suspicion.

Business purchaser

A good business plan can help you get a better price for your business. A purchaser is buying the assets and the future profits. The key part of the business the buyer is not getting is the current owner. The new owner is, however, probably going to inherit the management team if there is one. If it can be demonstrated that the business will happily run without the input of the owner, it becomes more valuable.

Emphasise the structure and systems that are in place and the relationships with customers which are not owner focused. If you have a solid strategy for steadily growing the business, that should be explained.

The financials are extremely important. The published accounts will probably be attached, but you will summarise the figures in the plan with possible explanations of performance. The forecast should be a natural progression of past performance: if it's not there had better be a good reason. If a business was seen to have the same turnover for the last three years, for example, a plan which showed a 10% growth on the forecast would be regarded with great suspicion. Unless a very good reason for the expected upturn was explained, all credibility could be lost.

This plan can be called a sales memorandum. It would be similar to a standard business plan apart from certain key points:

- 'Executive summary' can be called 'investment proposal'. It should summarise what you want the buyer to do, along with a description of the business and its main selling points.
- Do not include detailed strategy.
- Do not include people plans.
- Include the reason for selling.
- Emphasise what a great opportunity the investment affords but do not go over the top. It's very easy to lose credibility with over-optimistic forecasts.

Bear in mind the fact that the reader is highly likely to be a current or future competitor who is just fishing. Don't divulge any information that will be useful to a competitor until fairly late in the day. What you supply at first will not give buyers everything they need, but you can hold preliminary discussions on price, etc., before providing additional information. At the same time there is a need not to be over-secretive. If something isn't sensitive there is probably little point in holding it back.

Potential partner

More and more businesses are seeing the benefit of strategic alliances. This involves two or more organisations working together in a partnership. They may be from different parts of the supply chain or be direct competitors sharing resources. They may decide to share the investment in, say, a manufacturing plant for a new product, put their own badges on identical products and then compete aggressively in the marketplace.

Two businesses in the same field may have complementary strengths and together will become more than the sum of the parts. A strategic alliance often represents a much lower risk option than an acquisition, with each partner concentrating on what they are good at.

The plan will need to focus on the resources which the business is bringing to the table, emphasising the strengths of the firm which the other potential partner is lacking. Strategic alliances should not be dived into without adequate analysis and preparation.

Tender assessor

Most government contracts tend to be put out to tender these days, and a good business plan can reinforce a submission. The reader is looking for evidence of a track record and capability in the type of work described.

The plan should emphasise the resources that are available in the business. Readers like to be able to see evidence of back-up availability and possibly the ability to apply additional resources in the event of problems and delays.

Preparing tenders is very time consuming and a preliminary discussion will often determine whether or not you are actually in the frame. Once you know what is important to them, you can emphasise those resources in the plan.

Grant fund-holder

Sometimes a business plan will be requested to support a grant application. The key issue is the objective of the grant. Many are designed to boost local employment; many are designed to help the environment. Understand exactly what the aims are and focus on them. Estimate the number and type of jobs that will be created or protected, the amount of carbon emission that will be saved, the amount of landfill waste that will be recycled, etc. These facets need to feature prominently, especially in the executive summary.

IMPROVING BUSINESS PERFORMANCE

A good business plan will state the goals of the business and explain how they are going to be achieved. The business planning process determines the goals, develops the strategy for achieving them and communicates the aims throughout the organisation.

Through the process of cascading objectives, team meetings and staff appraisals, the whole process becomes dynamic and a fundamental element in the running of the business. The process is explained in detail in Chapter 12.

2
Structuring your business plan

The structure of a business plan is not set in stone. The plan is basically telling a story: the story of your business. It tells the reader where you have come from, where you are now and where you want to be. It also sets out what is needed at this present point in time and why.

The basic layout is a start point; it can easily be rearranged if that aids the flow of the story. Headings can be combined if there is little to say about some of them, and additional headings can be inserted as and when needed.

The plan must look professional. The look and feel create the enormously important first impression that the reader gets even before opening it. In this chapter we will look at how this can be achieved.

Be clear and concise. The readers of your plan are looking for quality rather than quantity. They are busy people and are likely to get annoyed by too much waffle. Take as much space as you need to get across the points you are trying to make, but keep it concise.

LAYING OUT THE COVER AND THE PAGES

Figures 2.1–2.3 suggest some sample layouts. The layout of the rest is as per the contents list. It shows the order in which the various topics could be covered in your plan. The contents list can be broken down into subheadings if desired.

Business Plan

Business Name

Date:

Copy Number:

This plan is for information ony and is not part of any offer of shares in the business or any other sales. Information is proprietary and confidential and may not be reproduced, disclosed or distributed without the written permission of _____.

Your *LOGO*

Figure 2.1   Cover layout

Your Business Name

Business Plan

Contact details

Name:

Position:

Address:

Telephone:

Email address:

Figure 2.2   Page 1 layout

Contents

Executive summary   Page _

Business description   Page _

Product/service   Page _

Target market   Page _

Competition   Page _

Strategy   Page _

Objectives   Page _

Marketing plan   Page _

Management   Page _

Operational plan   Page _

Financial plan   Page _

Exit plan   Page _

Appendices   Page _

Figure 2.3   Page 2 layout

ORGANISING THE CONTENT

Most business plans are 15–30 pages long, excluding appendices. Fewer than 10 pages would give an impression of lack of substance, while the business would have to be fairly complex for it to be more than 40.

Try not to make the appendices larger than the plan itself. There is no point in attaching everything you can think of – it will only annoy the reader. The following are a few guidelines about the wording of your plan:

- Edit your content for brevity. Eliminate unnecessary words. Financiers read many business plans and get annoyed by unnecessary padding. Use a simple business-like tone in your writing.
- Avoid slang, chattiness and industry buzz words. You may know what they mean but the reader may not.
- Avoid superlatives.
- Words such as best and brilliant often result in loss of credibility.
- Let the facts speak for themselves.
- Quoting third parties is always very powerful.
- Rather than 'Our aftersales service is the best in the business', it would be more powerful to say 'In last year's JD Sports reliability survey, we came top for aftersales service'.
- Bullet points are a good mechanism for highlighting facts.

EXECUTIVE SUMMARY

The executive summary goes first but is written last. Once you have completed your plan you have the challenge of condensing it into a page or two. By that, I really do mean two pages maximum!

Don't just cut and paste a few paragraphs. Write a synopsis which includes all the main points. Give it a lot of thought. Some readers don't get beyond the executive summary; you must sell them the idea of taking a bit more time to read the rest of it.

APPENDICES

The appendices are a useful home for material that would clutter up the plan. Include a brief summary and reference to the appendix number in the main text.

Hard information, such as a market report, can add credibility to forecasts you make.

Some examples of what can be included are:

- market research conclusions;
- technical details;
- letters of intent;
- CVs of key people;
- brochures;
- assumptions;
- photographs;
- organisation plan;
- production flowcharts;
- testimonials; and
- recent accounts.

INCORPORATING ILLUSTRATIONS

Graphs and charts can really make a plan come alive and you should be looking for the opportunity to use a few of them. Don't even think of trying to draw them by hand. Spreadsheet programs such as Excel have excellent graph-drawing facilities.

Line charts or bar charts are good to show something like sales over time, while you could try a pie chart for something like a product split.

Grab a graph from Excel

It is really very simple to get professional-looking graphs into your business plan. The following is an example of using Microsoft Excel, which is a very

	Turnover (£ millions)
2005	15.5
2006	16.3
2007	17.9
2008	19.4
2009	21.8
2010	23.6

Figure 2.4   Data for bar chart

popular program. First we will look at preparing a bar chart to show sales figures over the last few years. You could use a line graph but a bar chart may have more impact.

Diminish your 'business plan' Word document and open a blank Excel worksheet. Enter the years and corresponding turnovers into the Excel worksheet as shown in Figure 2.4. Leave the cell above the dates blank. Enter 'Turnover' above the sales figures as shown. Highlight the whole table and then click the Chart Wizard icon or **Insert→Chart**. The column design should already be highlighted, so just press **Finish** and your chart appears in your worksheet, complete with title. Now right click the legend box to the right of the chart and left click **Clear** as you don't need the key when charting a single set of data.

Right click white space on chart, left click **Copy**, enlarge Word, put the cursor where you want your chart and paste it into your business plan (see Figure 2.5). Voilà.

For something like product mix, use a pie chart. For example, if 25% of sales were from nuts in the last year, 35% were from bolts and 40% from washers, create the data table shown in Figure 2.6 in Excel.

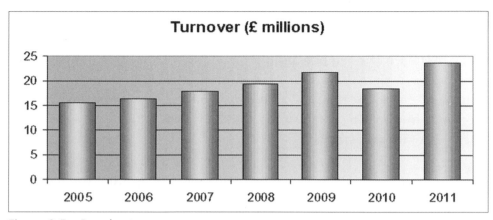

Figure 2.5   Bar chart

Nuts	Bolts	Washers
25%	35%	40%

Figure 2.6   Data for a pie chart

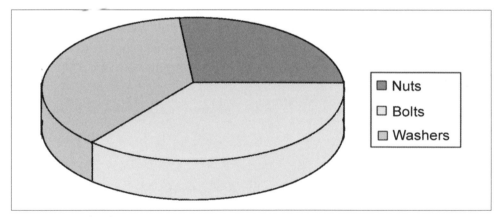

Figure 2.7   Pie chart

Highlight the whole table. **Insert→Chart**, choose **Pie** from list on left, click the second option in box on right to get a nice 3D effect, click **Finish**. Copy, **Paste** into your Word document (see Figure 2.7).

PRESENTATION

Always use A4 paper and only print it on one side. Don't cram too much on a sheet. Our preferred spacing has margin of at least 3 cm at the top and bottom, 2.5 cm on the right and a little more on the left to allow for binding. Use single-line spacing for text and the equivalent of at least double-line spacing between paragraphs.

Decide on your style for text, headings and subheadings from the start and stick to it. Changing the format halfway through the document would be very unprofessional.

Fonts

Modern word processors offer a large selection of fonts and the choice of appropriate ones is very important. Fonts fit into two categories: serif and sans serif.

Serif fonts are traditional newspaper type with thick and thin parts and little feet. They make reading easier and one of these would be the perfect choice for your text. Sans serif fonts have no fine lines or feet and are perfect for your headings. To play it safe go for a proven combination (see Table 2.1).

As this is a business document, keep to conventional, easy-to-read fonts and avoid anything too fancy.

Photographs

While you can insert one or two little photos in the plan itself, to make it more attractive, most of your photos should be in the appendices. You can show pictures of key products and your premises and that will give the plan

Table 2.1 Fonts and font sizes

Category	Font name	Font size
Main headings	Arial black	16 point
Sub headings	Arial black	14 point
Text	Times New Roman	12 point

vitality. Team photos aren't really necessary. If you are going to use photos, do make sure they are high quality; if they are not you will cheapen the plan. Photos and illustrations are best in colour if you have a suitable printer, but black and white will suffice.

Binding

Your business plan should be bound. Please don't use the cheap and nasty slide binders which won't allow the plan to sit flat on a desk. Use a comb-binding machine. They are pretty cheap now, but if you haven't got one, stationers such as Staples will bind the plan for you. Use good-quality paper and a nice cover.

Cover

A clear A4 plastic sheet is very popular as a cover. The first page can be read through it to give a professional effect. Alternatively print a coloured card cover. To look professional choose a dark blue or dark red card.

3

A sample plan

The following layout is a guide. The layout can be changed if desired, and subheadings can easily be combined where there isn't a lot of content. A plan may look as if it has little substance if there are a lot of subheadings with only a few words after each. The subheadings have been included here so that the layout can easily be followed, while maintaining brevity.

This is a sample of a level-1 *external plan for an established business.*

For an internal plan, add in functional objectives for the marketing, operations and management sections. These objectives should be part of the natural cascade from business to functional to personal. Create milestones from your one year objectives wherever appropriate, and review them at set intervals, typically quarterly. This process is described in Chapter 12.

For a start-up plan refer to Chapter 19, where there are detailed notes on adaptations to the sample.

Sample plan: level 1

1 EXECUTIVE SUMMARY

Maxigen is a profitable manufacturer of generators in the UK. The business has been established for over 30 years and turnover currently stands at £16 million.

The business is a private limited company which holds a patent for double spindle alternator technology. This technology reduces running costs significantly and represents a real competitive advantage.

We manufacture a wide range of portable engine-driven generators that are used widely in the construction industry. They provide reliable mains-type power where the electrical mains arc not available. We hold a 21% share of the UK market for this type of generator and have an excellent reputation for quality, reliability and aftersales service.

We now plan to expand by introducing a range of standby generators. These are permanently installed as a back up in buildings which have a mains supply. In the event of a power cut, the standby generator automatically switches in. There is a very big market for these units throughout the world, particularly in developing countries where the power supply is erratic. The technology used in the proposed range is very similar to the existing range and the new products can be distributed through channels that we already use. Resultantly we believe this initiative will be low risk.

Most of our existing products are sold direct to customers, with the largest sector being the plant and tool hire industry. We have a distributor network spanning much of western Europe, but it currently accounts for a small portion of our sales.

The market for back-up generators is slightly different. Users tend to buy them from distributors, the same distributors we currently deal with for our portable units. Our distributors have been encouraging us to enter the back-up market because our patented technology would deliver a powerful benefit to their customers.

We plan to increase our sales from £16 million to £18 million and generate a net profit of £588,000 for the year ending 31.3.14.

We will continue with our current highly successful marketing strategy of personal contact with our customers combined with exposure in exhibitions and advertising in the trade press.

We will, in addition to this, place an extra emphasis on developing our network of distributors to boost take up of our new range and plan to appoint one new distributor each month over the coming year.

Our workforce is highly skilled and run by an experienced management team headed up by our founders, Brian Jones and David Thomas.

The business operates out of a modern, well equipped, 20,000 sq ft factory in Coventry. Manufacturing is headed up by our Production Director, Peter Probert, who joined the company in 1979. Our production facility is fully ISO9000 registered and we are also a registered Investor in People.

We now need to increase our overdraft facility from £120,000 to £370,000 as the planned expansion will require more working capital. We will be purchasing new machinery for £1.2 million for which we will be using retained profits.

2   BUSINESS DESCRIPTION

Business details
- Business name: Maxigen Generators Ltd.
- Brand name: Maxigen.
- Address: Basildon Way, Kingswood Industrial Estate, Coventry.
- Telephone: 01234 123456.

- Websites: www.maxigen.co.uk.
- Email: info@maxigen.co.uk.
- Date founded: 1976.
- Turnover 2011/2012: £16 million.

Mission statement

Our goal is to increase our customers' efficiency by providing them with machines that are more reliable and cost less to run. We aim to be the European market leader in both the portable and back-up generator markets by 2020. We treat all our people with respect and invest heavily in their development. We treat customers as we would like to be treated.

Ownership, management and legal status

The business is a private limited company which holds a patent for double spindle alternator technology.

The business is owned by the three current executive directors:

- Brian Jones, Managing Director, 45%, joined 1976.
- David Thomas, Financial Director, 30%, joined 1976.
- Peter Probert, Production Director, 25%, joined 1979.

The other senior managers are as follows:

- Mary Jones, Sales and Marketing Manager, joined 1996.
- Jennifer Thompson, Human Resources Manager, joined 1994.

Including the above, the business employed 75 people on 20 January 2012.

Location

All production is carried out at the head office in Coventry.

Funding

Funding to date has come from the directors and bank loans. Currently £120,000 is owed to Barclays Bank plc. Due to planned expansion the business will need to boost its working capital and is now looking to increase its overdraft limit by £150,000 to £370,000. Capital expenditure for the expansion will be met through retained profits.

Achievements to date

The business is profitable, has a 21% market share in the UK and exports to seven other countries.

3 PRODUCTS AND SERVICES

The company manufactures a range of industrial generators. The Maxigen range provides portable power, with a wide range of applications, with the main one being construction sites. There is currently a range of six machines with outputs ranging from 50 KVa to 750 KVa. All our machines utilise the patented double spindle alternator system which results in a 26% fuel saving compared with the traditional technology used by our competitors.

Aftersales service is contracted out to specialist providers in all the countries we serve. We are able to guarantee a next-day call by a service engineer in any location. This is a better performance than the vast majority of our competitors are managing and an important factor in the excellent customer loyalty we enjoy.

We are now planning to start manufacturing a new range which will be called Maxigen Power Plus. These will be machines that are designed to provide back-up power generation which kicks in when mains power is lost. They will be permanently installed in buildings that need a back up in the case of mains failures.

The new range that we plan to develop will basically use the same technology as our existing machines and the manufacturing process will be virtually identical.

4 MARKET

Maxigen currently operates in western Europe. Geographical spread is:

- UK: 85%
- France: 4%

- Germany: 3%
- Benelux: 3%
- Spain: 3%
- Italy: 1%
- Ireland: 1%

We currently provide a full range of portable engine-driven power units.

The total UK market for engine driven portable generating sets up to 750 KVa in 2010 was estimated to be worth £155 million, while the European market was thought to be worth £450 million (Appendix XX).

Over the next five years the UK market is set to grow by an estimated 4% p.a., the European market by 6% p.a. and the worldwide market by 8% p.a.

We plan to introduce a new range of back-up generators in 2013. The market for back-up generators in Europe currently stands at £400 million and is growing at 12% p.a. That growth rate is expected to be maintained for the next five years (market report, Appendix XX).

There are also considerable opportunities in underdeveloped areas such as Africa, where the mains power supply is unreliable.

Target customers

The main sector for *portable engine-driven generators* is rental. For this reason the key target for Maxigen is UK rental companies. Service is more important than price to rental companies as their priority is keeping the fleet in service. In 2009 the UK plant and tool hire market was estimated to be worth £5 billion and is growing at 4%.

There are thousands of hire companies in the UK, but the top 10 held 29% of the market in 2009. For this reason we focus our efforts on the largest hire companies.

Back-up generators tend to be bought through distributors. We currently already have a network of four distributors in the UK, and one each in France, Germany, Benelux, Spain, Italy and Ireland who handle the Maxigen range. We have held discussions with our distributors and have discovered that they all currently sell back-up generators from competitors and are interested in handling our proposed new range as well.

5   COMPETITION

Maxigen (existing range)

In the portable engine-driven power market we estimate that we are number three in the UK out of around 25 suppliers. Our three major competitors are AAA Generators, BBB Generators (both larger than us) and DDD Generators (smaller than us).

The market leader, AAA Generators, has a good product, very low prices and an aftersales service which is below average. BBB has a slightly inferior product to AAA but good aftersales service and a slightly higher price. DDD has an average-quality product, average aftersales service and average price, which is approximately 5% more than BBB is charging.

Our products have excellent reliability, low running costs and customers rate our aftersales service as excellent (Appendix YY: HIA survey 2011). Resultantly we manage to command a price premium. We are the market leader in the hire sector because of the importance they place on reliability and aftersales service.

Our strategy will be to continue to focus on selling direct in the UK while increasing exports through the development of our distributor network.

Power Plus (new range)

We anticipate that our three main competitors in the back-up market will be AAA Generators, DDD Generators and EEE Generators. AAA is again the market leader with good products, low prices and poor aftersales service. DDD is average in everything, while EEE is very expensive and has very good service and an excellent product.

We plan to pitch our pricing at 10% below EEE. Our product is just as good, but our service will probably be slightly inferior and we will be newcomers to that part of the market.

Our strategy is to introduce three new machines of low to medium capacity. These machines represent more of the market than the larger ones do, are easier to manufacture and involve lower set-up costs.

6 STRATEGY

Our intention is to continue focusing on the major UK hire companies for the sale of our Maxigen range and to focus almost exclusively on our distributors for the new Power Plus range. Back-up generators are currently sold by all our major competitors mainly through distributors.

The key to success in both these markets is customer service. For the end user a generator is a critical item, breakdowns have to be addressed quickly and avoided whenever possible. The only way we can provide excellent customer service is through our people. Training and empowering our team so that decisions can be made on the spot will be a priority for us.

The greatest opportunity for growth lies with distributors and we will attempt to strengthen both our overseas and UK distributor networks.

Customer needs

Rental sector
Their primary requirements are for very reliable machines and excellent aftersales service. Our customer satisfaction survey has shown that for reliability they rate us at 70% and for service they rate us 88% (Appendix AA).

Distributors
Distributors are looking for a high margin on machines which are easy to sell. Our distributors have freedom to set their own prices, so margins do vary, but on average ours are typical for the industry. The end user is looking for a machine which is very reliable with low running costs. Our reliability is good and our running costs are lower due to the technology used. We are therefore confident that we can increase the amount of equipment supplied to distributors significantly.

Our distinctive competencies

We have been manufacturing generators for over 30 years and have a modern ISO9000 certified facility in the UK. Our patented technology gives significantly reduced running costs and our machines have proven to be very reliable. Our aftersales service is excellent, with an accredited network of aftersales service agents throughout Europe. We provide full training for the employees of our entire service network to ensure the maintenance of very high standards.

Weaknesses

Some competitors are significantly cheaper than us and have lower costs. They are, however, producing inferior machines and have lower levels of aftersales service.

Not being in the standby market has weakened our profile as distributors feel we don't have a full range, and some competitors have claimed that we lack the expertise to make machines of that type. Our new products will correct this weakness.

Strategy statement

The mainstay of the business is currently the large, UK rental companies and we will continue to give them the excellent service they require so that we may hold our position.

Our overall market standing is, we believe, currently being held back by the lack of standby units, as customers (particularly distributors) feel the range is incomplete. We plan to develop three new back-up models and introduce them into the market by September 2013.

We feel that distributors offer a significant opportunity for growth, both in the UK and overseas, as sales from that channel are significantly under-represented. We plan to increase the contact we have with existing distributors and actively attempt to recruit one new distributor a month over the coming year.

Risk factors

We may not find a market for the new machines

We are confident that there is an opportunity, as our existing customers are already buying these machines from competitors and have expressed an interest in getting their back-up machines from us. If they do fail to sell, we will very easily be able to utilise the additional capacity to build machines from our existing range.

The new machines may not work

The new products will use virtually the same technology successfully used in the existing range. We have the in-house expertise to sort out any teething troubles that may be experienced with the new machines.

There may be a downturn in the economy

Our biggest cost items are staff and raw materials. We can easily cut back on these to get us through a recession. In the event of a downturn we would make more effort to win additional market share in countries that were not so badly affected. The new range will actually strengthen our position in a key sector (distributors) in which we are currently weak. Winning additional market share in that sector could be our best insurance against a recession.

Taking a balanced view of our strategic position leads us to believe that investing in the business at this time represents a low-risk venture.

7 BUSINESS OBJECTIVES

Sales

Sales of £18 million for year ending 31 March 2014. This represents an increase of 12.5% on last year's figure of £16 million.

Net profit

A net profit of £588,000 represents a net margin of 1.5%, which is the same as it was last year.

Increase sales to hire sector to £12 millions for year to
31 March 2014
This has always been the key market for us. From a strong performance of
£11 million last year, we are looking for a modest growth that will in effect
see us holding our own.

Introduce 3 new Power Plus generators by 30 November 2013
New product development will need to be completed by 31 July 2013 so that
in-field testing can be carried out for three months before product launch.

Increase distributor network
One new distributor per month added and an increase of 5% in sales to
distributors for year to 31 March 2014.

8   MARKETING PLAN

We manufacture a wide range of engine-driven generators that are marketed
under the Maxigen brand. We are currently in the process of developing a
new range of small to medium sized, back-up generators that will form our
new Power Plus range.

Our prices are among the highest in the marketplace due to the high quality
of our products and exceptional aftersales service.

Over 90% of our output is currently distributed to the UK, with the rest
going into western Europe. We plan to grow our exports by developing our
distributor network.

We have set aside a promotional budget of £300,000 for the coming year and
that will be used in tradeshows, advertising in trade journals and two
direct-mail campaigns. Our sales force will also maintain close contact with
our direct key accounts and distribution network. This is the mix that we
have been using successfully for the last few years. The change will be to
place more emphasis on developing our distributor network.

We place a big emphasis on training. All sales people attend regular courses and
free training is provided for distributors and members of our service network.

9 MANAGEMENT AND SKILLS

Brian Jones, MBA, is Managing Director and started the business in 1976 with David Thomas, FCA, the current Financial Director. Prior to starting the business Brian had worked as UK Sales Manager for an Italian manufacturer of generators and David had worked for a national firm of chartered accountants.

Peter Probert joined the business in 1976 as a production assistant and since then has gradually worked his way up in the business. He was appointed as Production Director in 2006. His vast experience ensures that production moves smoothly and quality standards are maintained.

Mary Jones joined the business as a salesperson in 1996 and was appointed Sales and Marketing Manager in 2003. Her previous experience included ten years' sales and marketing experience in the telecommunications industry.

Jennifer Thompson, Human Resources Manager, joined in 1994 after five years' experience as Personnel Manager of HR Smith & Son, a bed manufacturer.

The management team has a cumulative experience in the company of over 100 years, and in those long years of service have honed the skills necessary to run the business successfully.

There is a clear management structure in place (Appendix XXX). Some 75 people work for the business, with average length of service being 12.4 years. The workforce is highly skilled. Everyone agrees a training plan each year and is empowered to make decisions. The culture of the business is very supportive and respects staff, customers and suppliers.

We are planning to build back-up machines and have no one with specific experience of doing that, so we will recruit an engineer with that background to supplement our team.

10 OPERATIONS

The business operates from a 20,000 sq ft factory at Coventry. The company is well equipped, with modern machinery and its quality control system is ISO9000 registered.

Over the years the business has invested heavily in equipment and now enjoys the benefit of a very efficient production process. Stock levels and the amount of work in progress have been reduced significantly in recent years through the introduction of just in time. We have worked very closely with our key suppliers to implement the system successfully and it now works very well.

We plan to increase capacity so that the new machines can be introduced. We have enough factory space for this but will need to purchase four new machines (Appendix AAA) and recruit five additional workers.

The business operates on a single shift system with overtime being worked by most workers on Saturdays and Sundays. This is a very flexible approach as costs can easily be cut, if orders fall back, by reducing overtime.

11 FINANCIALS

The company's financial details are set out in Figures 3.1–3.5.

Assumptions

These forecasts are based on the assumption that the economy remains at its current level and that there are no significant changes in the level of competition.

12 EXIT PLAN

We need to increase the overdraft facility to £370,000 for two years, after which a level of £250,000 should suffice, as a proportion of profits will be set aside towards working capital.

In three years' time we plan to enter the AIM market. This will give us an injection of capital to fund further growth, and enable the current shareholders to liquidise some of their investment.

Maxigen
Projected Profit and Loss   Year 1   £ thousands

	Jan	Feb	Mar	Apr	May	Jun	Jul	Aug	Sep	Oct	Nov	Dec	Total
SALES	1500	1500	1500	1500	1800	1200	1200	1000	1800	2000	1500	1500	18000
COST OF SALES													0
Materials	450	450	450	450	540	360	360	300	540	600	450	450	5400
Direct labour	375	375	375	375	450	300	300	250	450	500	375	375	4500
Distribution	75	75	75	75	90	60	60	50	90	100	75	75	900
Commissions	75	75	75	75	90	60	60	50	90	100	75	75	900
TOTAL COST OF SALES	975	975	975	975	1170	780	780	650	1170	1300	975	975	11700
GROSS PROFIT	525	525	525	525	630	420	420	350	630	700	525	525	6300
GROSS PROFIT %	35	35	35	35	35	35	35	35	35	35	35	35	420
OVERHEADS													0
Indirect wages and salaries	400	400	400	400	400	400	400	400	400	400	400	400	4800
Directors remuneration	25	25	25	25	25	25	25	25	25	25	25	25	300
Premises costs	23	23	23	23	23	23	23	23	23	23	23	23	276
Office costs	9	9	9	9	9	9	9	9	9	9	9	9	108
Travel	11	11	11	11	11	11	11	11	11	11	11	11	132
Sundries	2	2	2	2	2	2	2	2	2	2	2	2	24
Bank costs	4	4	4	4	4	4	4	4	4	4	4	4	48
Depreciation	2	2	2	2	2	2	2	2	2	2	2	2	24
TOTAL	476	476	476	476	476	476	476	476	476	476	476	476	5712
NET PROFIT/LOSS	49	49	49	49	154	−56	−56	−126	154	224	49	49	588
NET MARGIN %	3.3	3.3	3.3	3.3	8.6	−4.7	−4.7	−12.6	8.6	11.2	3.3	3.3	2.1
CUMULATIVE b/f	0	49	98	147	196	350	294	238	112	266	490	539	
CUMULATIVE c/f	49	98	147	196	350	294	238	112	266	490	539	588	

Figure 3.1   Projected profit and loss, year 1

Maxigen
Projected Profit and Loss

	Year 2					Year 3				
	Quarter 1	Q2	Q3	Q4	Total 13	Q1	Q2	Q3	Q4	Total 14
SALES	5000	6000	4500	5000	20500	5500	6500	5000	5500	22500
COST OF SALES					0					0
Materials	1500	1800	1350	1500	6150	1650	1950	1500	1650	6750
Direct labour	1250	1500	1125	1250	5125	1375	1625	1250	1375	5625
Distribution	250	300	225	250	1025	275	325	250	275	1125
Commissions	250	300	225	250	1025	275	325	250	275	1125
TOTAL COST OF SALES	3250	3900	2925	3250	13325	3575	4225	3250	3575	14625
GROSS PROFIT	1750	2100	1575	1750	7175	1925	2275	1750	1925	7875
GROSS PROFIT %	35	35	35	35	140	35	35	35	35	140
OVERHEADS					0					0
Indirect wages and salaries	1400	1400	1400	1400	5600	1600	1600	1600	1600	6400
Directors remuneration	100	100	100	100	400	100	100	100	100	400
Premises costs	75	75	75	75	300	75	75	75	75	300
Office costs	30	30	30	30	120	30	30	30	30	120
Travel	36	36	36	36	144	36	36	36	36	144
Sundries	8	8	8	8	32	8	8	8	8	32
Bank costs	15	15	15	15	60	15	15	15	15	60
Depreciation	8	8	8	8	32	8	8	8	8	32
TOTAL	1672	1672	1672	1672	6688	1872	1872	1872	1872	7488
NET PROFIT/LOSS	78	428	−97	78	487	53	403	−122	53	387
NET MARGIN %	1.6	7.1	−2.2	1.6	2.4	1.0	6.2	−2.4	1.0	5.687273
CUMULATIVE b/f	588	666	1094	997		1075	1128	1531	1409	
CUMULATIVE c/f	666	1094	997	1075		1128	1531	1409	1462	

Figure 3.2 Projected profit and loss years 2 and 3

Maxigen
Projected Cash Flow

	Jan	Feb	Mar	Apr	May	Jun	Jul	Aug	Sep	Oct	Nov	Dec	Total
						Year 1							
INCOME													
SALES	1300	1500	1500	1500	1500	1800	1200	1200	1000	1800	2000	1500	17800
Issue of shares													0
Loans													0
VAT reclaim													0
TOTAL INCOME	1300	1500	1500	1500	1500	1800	1200	1200	1000	1800	2000	1500	17800
OUTLAY													
Capital expenditure													0
Materials	300	300	300	300	300	300	300	300	300	300	300	300	3600
Direct labour	375	375	375	375	450	300	300	250	450	500	375	375	4500
Distribution	75	75	75	75	90	60	60	50	90	100	75	75	900
Commissions	75	75	75	75	90	60	60	50	90	100	75	75	900
Overheads (less depreciation)	474	474	474	474	474	474	474	474	474	474	474	474	5688
Corporation tax													0
Loan repayments	5	5	5	5	5	5	5	5	5	5	5	5	60
TOTAL OUTLAY	1304	1304	1304	1304	1409	1199	1199	1129	1409	1479	1304	1304	15648
NET CASH FLOW	−4	196	196	196	91	601	1	71	−409	321	696	196	
OPENING CASH b/f	−4	−4	192	388	584	675	1276	1277	1348	939	1260	1956	
CUMULATIVE CASH c/f	−4	192	388	584	675	1276	1277	1348	939	1260	1956	2152	

Figure 3.3 Projected cash flow, year 1

Maxigen
Projected Cash Flow

	Year 2					Year 3				
	Quarter 1	Q2	Q3	Q4	Total Yr 2	Q1	Q2	Q3	Q4	Total Yr 3
INCOME										
SALES	5000	5000	6000	4500	20500	5000	5500	6500	5000	22000
Issue of shares					0					0
Loans					0					0
VAT reclaim					0					0
TOTAL INCOME	5000	5000	6000	4500	20500	5000	5500	6500	5000	22000
OUTLAY										
Capital expenditure					0					0
Materials	1000	1000	1200	900	4100	1000	1100	1300	1000	4400
Direct labour	1250	1250	1500	1125	5125	1250	1375	1625	1250	5500
Distribution	250	250	300	225	1025	250	275	325	250	1100
Commissions	250	250	300	225	1025	250	275	325	250	1100
Overheads (less depreciation)	1664	1664	1664	1664	6656	1664	1664	1664	1664	6656
Corporation tax					0					0
Loan repayments	15	15	15	15	60	15	15	15	15	60
TOTAL OUTLAY	4429	4429	4979	4154	17991	4429	4704	5254	4429	18816
NET CASH FLOW	571	571	1021	346		571	796	1246	571	3184
OPENING CASH b/f	2152	2723	3294	4315		4661	5232	6028	7274	
CUMULATIVE CASH c/f	2723	3294	4315	4661		5232	6028	7274	7845	

Figure 3.4 Projected cash flow, years 2 and 3

Maxigen
Projected Balance sheets

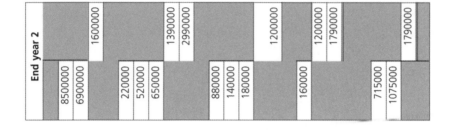

	End year 1		End year 2		End year 3	
FIXED ASSETS						
Cost	8500000		8500000		8500000	
Depreciation	6500000		6900000		7200000	
Total fixed assets		2000000		1600000		1300000
CURRENT ASSETS						
Stock	200000		220000		230000	
Debtors	500000		520000		550000	
Cash at bank	650000		650000		680000	
Total current assets		1350000		1390000		1460000
Total Assets		3350000		2990000		2760000
CURRENT LIABILITIES						
Trade creditors	850000		880000		900000	
Tax payable	120000		140000		160000	
Short term loans	120000		180000		170000	
Total current liabilities		1090000		1200000		1230000
LONG TERM LIABILITIES						
Loans	50000		160000		140000	
Total liabilities		1090000		1200000		1230000
Net Assets		2260000		1790000		1530000
Represented by						
Shareholders capital	1672000		715000		68000	
Profit and Loss a/c	588000	2260000	1075000	1790000	1462000	1530000

Figure 3.5   Balance sheet

4

Market

Before you can begin to plan effectively, you must understand the market you are operating in and any markets you plan to enter. You will be defining the market, explaining how it works, and saying why you have chosen the specific target within that market you have.

Why you need it

Any funder is interested in the size and nature of the market you are aiming at because with no idea of the size of the market, forecasting can be seen as pie in the sky. It is also important when making internal plans to have an idea of how big the pie, which you are sharing with your competitors, is.

Market: level 1

SEGMENTING YOUR MARKET

First of all define the market you are in and explain how it works. The overall market is going to be quite big and may cover the whole world. As you will probably only be occupying a small part of the market, you will need to break it down. This process is called segmentation (Figure 4.1).

Segmenting your market will increase the impact of your marketing. Trying to sell your offering to everybody who could possibly buy it would make little impact unless you had a massive marketing budget, and even then it wouldn't be very clever. Instead, focus your effort on the buyers you are best able to serve. If you think of all possible buyers as a big cake, you should be aiming for a particular slice.

Define exactly what part of the market you are operating in, any new parts you plan to enter and the geographical area you will be covering.

Example

If you are a builder, constructing new houses between the value of £150,000 and £300,000 within a 25 mile radius of Reading, your market is construction. That can be segmented down to house building, further segmented to a £150,000–£300,000 price range and further again segmented to a 25-mile radius of Reading.

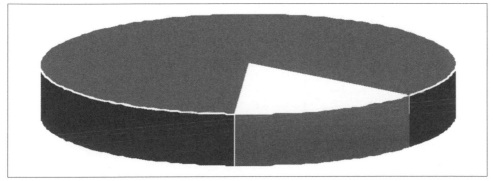

Figure 4.1   Segmentation

CHOOSING YOUR TARGET

All businesses have customers and potential customers that form the market they operate in. Those customers are all different but share certain characteristics. It's these common characteristics that we are interested in. Once you start looking for these common characteristics, you will soon realise that your customers fit quite neatly into groups. Understanding these groups will help you make the most of your marketing budget.

When you think about it, some of the groups represent a much higher proportion of your turnover than others. Some of them are more profitable than others. Complete the customer analysis worksheet in Figure 4.2 to help you decide who your target market will be. Don't try to be too accurate here. In-depth analysis is not required. We are just looking for a general feel.

Example

If a manufacturer sells car parts to retailers, wholesalers, garages and the general public, these are clearly the four basic groups.

The retailer group has 30 customers and the total sales value from them was £500,000. Enter £500,000 under sales value for the retail group.

Estimate the average gross margin from the group. If you are selling your product to the group for an average of £100, and the direct costs involved (cost of product including direct labour) are £70, then you have a gross margin of 30%.

Group	Group description	No. of customers	Sales value (if available)	Gross margin	Advantages	Dis-advantages
1						
2						
3						
4						

Our target market will be:
1. Customers:
2. Location:

Figure 4.2   Customer analysis worksheet

Now determine the main advantages and disadvantages of dealing with the group. For the retailer group the main advantage may be high volume while the main disadvantage could be low margins.

Repeat for the other groups. After analysing, you may be surprised to discover who your most desirable customers are.

Customer needs

Different things are often important to different groups of customers. All businesses have strengths and weaknesses. You are far more likely to succeed with a group whose primary needs are for things you are good at. It would be folly to concentrate on customers who value highly the parts of the overall package that you are weakest in.

Don't just assume you know what the needs of the various customer groups are – ask them (see Figure 4.3)! Compare the results with your SWOT (Chapter 9).

Now make a choice using the results of your worksheets. Which groups would you like more of and are there any groups would you prefer not to have? It sounds radical, but some groups may be costing you money to serve. In other words, the profits you are making from 'good' customers can be going to support 'bad' customers.

The groups you want to focus on are your target market. Your target market is all the potential customers with the characteristics you have discovered, located within the area you have decided to serve.

Group	Group description	Primary needs
1		
2		
3		
4		

Figure 4.3   Customer needs worksheet

Choosing geographical spread is a key strategic decision. Naturally the bigger the geographic spread, the more target customers you find, but the more difficult they are to serve. You may however decide that going further geographically is easier than increasing market share in your existing territory.

Attacking too wide a market too soon will consume an inordinate amount of resource, while being over-cautious will result in missed opportunities that others may seize. You do need a balance.

In your business plan builder (see Figure 4.4) describe the groups you are aiming at and the geographic area you will be covering.

CHANNELS

Explain the logistics of your market. Are there lots of small competitors covering your area or just a couple of large ones? What are the distribution channels? Describe how materials are supplied. Is there a wide choice of suppliers or just one or two very powerful ones? Are you supplying wholesalers, retailers or the end user directly?

What is the norm in the industry and is your approach any different?

ASSESSING THE SIZE OF THE MARKET AND FUTURE TRENDS

Try getting in touch with your trade association, and ask them what size the market is now, how it is forecasted to grow over the next three years and

Market
Definition
Segmentation
Target
Channels
Size of market and source
Future trends

Figure 4.4   Market plan builder, level 1

what the growth rate has been over the last two to three years. If you don't know the name of the relevant trade association try using a search engine.

You will probably find your trade association helpful even if you are not a member. They will probably only be able to give you figures for countries as a whole. To convert this to a local figure, ask the Economic Development Department of the relevant local authority what the percentage GDP of their area is, compared with the country as a whole. Then simply multiply the national figure by that percentage.

Don't forget to state in your plan where the figures came from. Alternative sources of information are Business Links and local libraries.

TOP TIP

If you are saying little under each subheading, your plan could look neater if you try just using the market structure main heading and explain the points without subheadings.

Market: level 2

Suitability

You have experience of business planning and external analysis and feel ready to take a step forward from level 1. Remember you do not have to be at the same level for all parts of the plan and should incorporate level 1 into your planning.

Definition, segmentation and channels

These are basically as described in level 1, but your description should probably show more detail.

Target

Spend a little more time thinking about your different customer groups. Ask yourself how attractive each is and weigh up the advantages and disadvantages of dealing with each group from your point of view.

Some customers are a lot more troublesome than others. Why is that so? Do you put up with it because you make more profit from them or they spend a lot? Surprisingly many businesses find out on analysis that the troublesome customers actually cost the company money rather than provide profit. Use the customer analysis worksheet in level 1 (Figure 4.2) to carry out this analysis, working to a higher level of detail than you did at level 1.

It should become obvious which type of customer you would like to win more of, so put them in your target market.

Size of the market

Estimating the size of your market can be tricky for a small business. Published data are often not very helpful as they may cover a wider market than is being operated in and possible a larger geographic area. There are various ways that can be used to estimate it in addition to the method described in level 1.

To get a rough estimate of your market size, ask yourself how many competitors you have in your area. How do they compare with you size-wise, on average? You probably don't know their turnover but you probably do know roughly how many operatives they have in your area. You know what your turnover is, so from the above you can make a rough and ready estimation of your market size.

Example 1

There are 19 competitors and your business is about average size. Your turnover is £500,000 and as you are one of 20, and of average size, your share is $\frac{1}{20}$ of the market. Market size is therefore £500,000 × 20 = £10 million:

Your turnover = 500,000
Average turnover = 500,000
As there are 20 players, 500,000 is $\frac{1}{20}$ of the market

Market size = 500,000 × 20 = *£10,000,000*

Example 2

If your business is bigger or smaller than average size you have to make an adjustment. If you estimated your business to be, say, two thirds the size of the average competitor in your area, your turnover was £300,000 and you had nine competitors:

Your turnover = 300,000
Average turnover = 450,000 (300,000 × $\frac{3}{2}$)
As there are 10 players, 450,000 is $\frac{1}{10}$ of the market

Market size = 450,000 × 10 = *£4,500,000*

Your *market share* is $\dfrac{300,000}{4,500,000} \times 100 = 6.6\%$

Alternative method

Ask your suppliers what the size of your market is. They will know how many units they are supplying into your area and probably have a good idea of what their share of the market is. You will probably need to persuade your contact to get the figures from their marketing department. Once you know how many units are going into your market in total and how many units you are shifting, you have your rough market size.

This gives your approximate share of the market based on units installed. As long as each unit is sold for an average market place price, it will also give your market share in monetary terms which is more significant.

Example

You install central heating systems. The key product is the boiler. Each competitor will be installing some as replacement boilers and some as part of a new system. The differing shares of new to replacement will cause inaccuracy as the proportions will vary, but *number of boilers fitted* is still a good indication of market size.

If your supplier has estimated that 5,000 boilers a year are going into your area, and you are fitting 750 boilers a year then you have:

$$\frac{750}{5,000} \times 100 = 15\% \text{ market share}$$

If your turnover is £15,000,000, your *market* size is:

$$\frac{15,000,000}{15} \times 100 = £100,000,000$$

Future trends

Your suppliers probably have a good idea of how the market will grow over the next few years. Ask them what they think it will be.

Try also asking a few of your main customers what their spending expectations are.

Market
Definition
Segmentation
Target
Channels
Size of market
Our market share
Future trends

Figure 4.5   Market plan builder, level 2

Market: level 3

At level 3 you should have a much wider understanding of your market and how everything within it operates. Collect information from as many sources as you can and complete all the worksheets in detail to help you get as complete a picture as possible. This will form the basis from which your team will be able to identify both opportunities and threats.

UNDERSTANDING THE BUSINESS ENVIRONMENT

A business does not operate in a vacuum. It has to contend with powerful external forces over which it has little or no control. Together they have a massive effect on the ease with which the business can go about its day-to-day trading. They can trigger great riches or complete annihilation. The forces are in a constant state of flux. They vary from area to area, country to country, and time to time. It pays to keep an eye on them.

The economy

How your business will be affected by the economy must be analysed and explained. Potential periods of recession and boom must be planned for.

For example, a good recession plan can be the difference between survival or not. It is far more effective to plan for a recession before it starts, as then it will be done objectively, rather than with the panic which can cloud thinking once the business is in trouble.

Economies seem to go through an unending pattern of ups and downs or booms and busts. The global nature of business often results, now, in the whole world being affected by the same cycle.

There are four main phases to the cycle:

■   **Boom:** high levels of consumer spending, business confidence, investment and profits create a general feeling of well-being and affluence. Unemployment is low but there is pressure on inflation.

- **Recession:** the contraction of the economy dents confidence and that causes a cutback in investment, unemployment rises and consumer spending falls.

- **Depression:** the recession tends to spiral downwards if unchecked because its individual factors each make the other parts worse. If it goes on for too long it becomes a depression. Business confidence goes through the floor, unemployment grows further and prices can start to fall. Deflation reduces investment even further. Many businesses fail during this phase.

- **Recovery:** as things start to improve, people start spending more, businesses start to invest again and unemployment starts to fall gradually.

Figure 4.6 shows clearly the recession of 2008/9 and how the whole world was affected.

How the economy will change in the future is a key determiner of your future prosperity. Not all businesses are equally affected however. For most businesses a recession is very bad news.

Some businesses thrive in a recession. Low-price retailers such as Lidl see an increase in customers, as do fast-food outlets such as McDonald's. The low-cost alternatives do well as people tighten their belts.

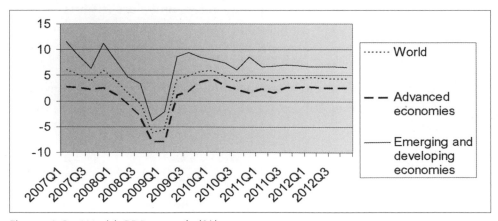

Figure 4.6   World GDP growth (%)

Other factors

There are other forces out there that warrant keeping an eye on as they could well have an effect on your business performance and provide opportunities or threats:

- **Social**: are people changing their beliefs and the way they behave? Examples are the increase in single-parent families and the greater health consciousness which led to the rise in popularity of wholefoods.
- **Technological**: innovative new products and improved production techniques have had a considerable effect on the business landscape in recent years and the rate of change seems to be increasing.
- **Political**: government policy is continually changing. This has both negative and positive effects on businesses. New laws can make trading more difficult, taxes can go up and down, while grants come and go.

A good source of data is the National Statistical Office. You can get trends for the UK as a whole, and certain particular industry trends, free of charge. (Figure 4.7 gives a business environment worksheet.)

INDUSTRY ANALYSIS AND TRENDS

Your industry consists of everyone involved in the supply of similar products and services to yours, including the whole supply chain from maker to retailer. You are all bound by a set of forces unique to your 'industry'. Understanding your industry is essential if you want to create a meaningful

Indicator	Three-year forecast	Impact on business
GDP growth Interest rates Inflation Exchange rates: £ to € £ to $ Unemployment Legislation Social, including green issues		

Figure 4.7   Business environment worksheet

plan. You may, of course, be operating in more than one industry. If that is the case you will need an understanding of each.

Industries are generally big animals and it's quite easy to find out how they are behaving from generally available statistics. Finding a forecast for your industry will be very useful when it comes to planning the future of your business. It will tell you how you can expect your business to perform if you do not gain or lose market share. If your intention is to gain market share, the industry forecast is your start point.

Try to get hold of a market report such as one of those produced by Mintel or Keynote. It can tell you the size of the overall market and what the forecasts are for the near future. On the downside there may not be a report available for your market, it may cover a market so much wider than the one you are operating in that it becomes meaningless, or it may be out of date.

Economic cycle

The performance of most industries follows the economic cycle (see above) quite closely. Some are affected more than most (e.g. construction), while some can actually benefit from a downturn (e.g. cheap fast food). Explain how the cycle affects your business and how you will respond to it.

Seasonality

If you sell ice cream on the beach you will know that business is not too good in the winter, while Father Christmases will find work hard to come by in the summer. While these are extreme examples, many businesses find sales to be better at certain times of the year than others. It can put severe pressure on cash flow and should be taken into account in your plan.

Sensitivity to regulations

All industries have to comply with government regulations but, for some, they are more significant than to others. Environmental legislation has made life difficult for natural polluters, while health and safety, employment protection, fair trade, etc., can have wide-ranging effects. Consider which regulations have an effect on your business. Do you need to make any changes because of them?

Supply and distribution

In some industries there are small numbers of powerful suppliers while in others it is difficult to gain access to distribution channels. It can be a significant barrier to entry, which does protect you from new entrants if you are already in the market, but does hand a degree of control of your business to suppliers/distributors.

Are there any changes you can make to strengthen your position in the supply chain? (Figure 4.8 gives an industry worksheet.)

	Actual performance			Forecast	
	Year before last	Last year	This year	Next year	Following year
UK market revenue Growth rate %					

Figure 4.8   Industry worksheet

Strategic opportunities

Having developed a greater understanding of the playing field, it is now time to think in very general terms where the main opportunities are. This does not mean that you will pursue them all, but does show that you understand what they are. This will also form a springboard to subsequent strategic planning.

Brainstorm what you have found out about your market along with what you already know to identify a couple of possible opportunities for your business and describe them (see Figure 4.9).

Market
Definition
The business environment
Industry analysis
Segmentation
Target
Channels
Size of market
Our market share
Future trends
Strategic opportunities

Figure 4.9   Market plan builder, level 3

5

Assessing the competition

Don't make the mistake of believing that you have no competitors. This is especially true of a new venture. If there really is no competition there is probably no market. Even if you have developed an exciting new product with brand-new technology, the like of which has never been seen before, you still need to be solving a problem for your customer. How is the customer currently solving that problem? There is your competitor!

Why you need it

You will be more likely to gain the confidence of lenders if they believe you understand whom you are up against. Strategic planning revolves around winning customers from competitors. The more you know about them the more confidently you can plan how to beat them. The plan should show how you are going to make yourself more attractive to customers and win more business from your competitors.

The competition: level 1

Competition comprises:

- **Direct competitors:** suppliers similar to yourself.
- **Indirect competitors:** often offering substitute products (the new producers of electric light bulbs were competitors to the old candle-making industry).

UNDERSTANDING COMPETITORS

List your major competitors. Just three or four should be enough. Now, how much do you know about them? In each case jot down the main ways in which they are better than you and the main ways in which they are inferior to you.

Some competitors are more of a threat than others. If a strong player is intent on winning more of the market, the rest have a problem. The more you know about your main competitors the better. If you understand exactly how they are better than you and how they are worse than you, you have already taken the first step towards strengthening your competitive position.

Strengths and weaknesses

Involve your team, especially salespeople. Try to think of this from the customers' point of view. Generally, for example, if competitors have lower prices, that's a weakness for you. If they are not making any money that's a strength for you, as they are financially weaker.

CREATING YOUR STRATEGY

It's time for you and your team to use what you have concluded to try to work out what you need to change to win more business from each competitor. In each case, try to determine the one thing that will make the most difference. In other words you are trying to strengthen your competitive edge (see Figure 5.1).

The competition
Competitor A
Name
Main strengths
Main weaknesses
Strategy
Competitor B
Name
Main strengths
Main weaknesses
Strategy
Competitor C
Name
Main strengths
Main weaknesses
Strategy

Figure 5.1   Competition plan builder, level 1

TOP TIP

Try to base competitors' strengths and weaknesses on your own performance. Strengths are things they do better than you. Weaknesses are things they do worse than you. Strategy is the change planned to strengthen your position.

The competition: level 2

Suitability

You have experience of business planning and external analysis and feel ready to take a step forward from level 1. Remember you do not have to be at the same level for all parts of the plan.

Competitors

List your major competitors. Discuss with your whole team what exactly you know about them. Different members of your group will know different things about each competitor. Create a file for each major competitor. When information is collated from everybody, you will be surprised at just how much you do know about them, and now everyone will have access to it.

Extend your knowledge by looking in their websites and gathering brochures, price lists, etc. Visit their showrooms, exhibition stands, etc. It is even possible to gain knowledge from suppliers and customers, but diplomacy will be needed.

Main strengths and weaknesses

Use your new-found knowledge to strengthen your analysis and list them as previously described at level 1.

Creating your strategy

As level 1.

Business plan builder

Use the level-1 form.

The competition: level 3

Competitors

Obtain the accounts of your major competitors and carry out a financial analysis. You may choose to get your accountant to help you do this, but you will gain a better internal understanding if a team member can do it.

To get the accounts of a UK limited company, go to the Companies House website and search for the particular competitor. If they are small, they will probably have submitted abbreviated accounts which will not have a profit and loss account included. It only costs a few pounds for each one so it's probably worth a try. Even abbreviated accounts are useful as they contain the balance sheet information.

There are a number of things that you should probably compare.

Net profit

This is at the bottom of the profit and loss (P & L) page. It is the amount of money made or lost in the year.

Gross Profit

Found in the P & L. This is profit before indirect costs are taken off. This shows what the margin is and gives an indication of how easily the business can be scaled up.

Debt

Balance sheet. Look at how much they owe. Add the less than one-year creditors to the more than one-year creditors. Competitors with a lot of debt may well be vulnerable.

Financial ratios

These are the essential indicators of the overall financial condition of an organisation. Liquidity ratios measure the availability of cash. Activity ratios measure the speed with which non-cash assets are converted to cash. Debt ratios measure ability to repay what is owed. Profitability ratios show how much money the firm is making.

Examples

Measure of performance

$$\text{Profit margin} = \frac{\text{Profit before interest and tax}}{\text{Sales}}$$

This is a key indicator. It shows in effect how much trading profit is being made for each pound of sales. The higher the percentage the stronger the business.

Measure of solvency

$$\text{Debt ratio} = \frac{\text{Long-term debt}}{\text{Capital employed}}$$

Shows what proportion of the money the business is using has been borrowed. The lower the figure, the stronger the competitor.

Measure of liquidity

$$\text{Acid test} = \frac{\text{Liquid assets}}{\text{Current liabilities}}$$

This is the strictest liquidity test. It calculates the short-term resources available to meet short-term liabilities. If the figure is less than 1 the competitor may be in trouble. The higher the figure, the stronger the liquidity of the business is.

Financial strength is a key competitive advantage as it can create options unavailable to competitors.

Main strengths and weaknesses

This financial information should strengthen the analysis. Carry out a similar financial analysis on your own business and compare your findings with your competitors.

Creating your strategy

Outline the possible competitive strategies that could be used against each competitor, bearing in mind that financially weaker opponents are less likely to be able to withstand a frontal attack than stronger ones and will have fewer options open to them. (Figure 5.2 gives a level-3 competitor plan builder.)

The competition
Competitor A
Name
Financial analysis
Main strengths
Main weaknesses
Strategy
Competitor B
Name
Financial analysis
Main strengths
Main weaknesses
Strategy
Competitor C
Name
Financial analysis
Main strengths
Main weaknesses
Strategy

Figure 5.2   Competitor plan builder, level 3

6

Business description

The business description helps the reader understand your business. It explains where you are now and where you have come from. This section is fairly easy to complete, but it still requires a lot of thought.

A key reason for business underperformance is a lack of in-depth understanding by management teams of their businesses. A common effect is a lack of focus, which often leads to inappropriate diversifications and acquisitions that usually go wrong.

Why you need it

If an investor cannot understand a business, no investment is made. A clear, concise business description tells readers what they need to know and critically demonstrates that you understand the business yourself. In fact, completing this section will probably deepen your understanding of the business in itself.

YOUR BUSINESS NAME

State the full legal name of the business. There may, however, be additional names that can be mentioned. Is the business trading under a different name? If so, state 't/a your trading name'. Mention any brand name which is different from the business name. If there are subsidiary businesses, list them. Also indicate the domain name of the business.

LEGAL

Indicate the legal structure of the business. Are you a sole trader, a partnership, a private limited company, a public limited company, a co-operative, a charity, etc.?

Do you have any licensing agreements, distribution agreements, trademarks, patents, etc.? Ensure they are all mentioned.

OWNERSHIP

List the owners with their percentage holding.

LISTING THE MANAGEMENT

List the chairperson, managing director and other key members of the management team. If there is a board of directors, indicate how often it meets and how many members there are. Listing the names of the individual directors is optional. If any of the names are likely to be recognised by the reader it would probably be good to include the full list.

GIVING THE LOCATION

Enter the address of the business head office. If there are branches include those addresses as well. If there are more than three or four branches simply state the number and include the list in an appendix.

Tell the reader where your customers are. Simply describe the geographic area the business covers – e.g. 'we cover the whole of the UK but 95% of our customers are located within a 30-mile radius of Reading'.

FUNDING TO DATE

Explain how the business has been funded to date. This could include:

- investment by directors;
- investment by others;
- loans from banks, etc;
- directors' loans; and
- loans from suppliers, customers, etc.

Explain any major financial obligations of the business and the terms of loans and investments.

What funding is now needed by the business and what will it be used for?

ACHIEVEMENTS TO DATE

This is a very important item as it shows the reader what progress has been made so far and that builds confidence. Examples are the build-up of sales and profits, successful introduction of new products, build-up of customer list, etc. Even a start up has a record of accomplishments – the product range may have been developed, a patent may have been obtained, distributors may have been lined up, etc.

Indicate where the business is in its development. The key stages are often described as follows:

- **Pre-start up**: you haven't launched yet.
- **Start up**: you are in your first year of trading.
- **Growth**: you are introducing new products or services, widening your area of operation or increasing market share.
- **Recovery**: you are turning around from a poor position.
- **Established**: the business is mature and revenue streams are steady.

Figure 6.1 gives a business description plan builder.

TOP TIP

Think hard about your achievements to date as they really do impress readers. Ask your team what they think your achievements are.

Business description
Legal name
Trading names
Subsidiaries
Websites
Company number
Date of inception
Legal structure
Ownership
Management
Head office address
Head office telephone number
Branches
Achievements to date
Funding to date
Funding requirement

Figure 6.1   Business description plan builder

7
Describing your products and services

For the purpose of business planning, products and services can essentially be treated in the same way. The fundamental difference between them is that products can be made and then kept for sale at a later date. The value of a service, however, is lost if it is not sold immediately. As an example, if an airline seat is not sold before the plane takes off, its value for that flight is completely lost.

In principle, the products and services section does not need to be very long. There is no need, as such, to go into a massive amount of detail. If the section is short, it can be tucked into the business description section under a products and services subheading. One of the main purposes of many plans, however, is to gain approval or funding for the development of a new product or service or to boost capacity in an existing one. In that case, the product and service part will be a key component of the plan and will undoubtedly need a section of its own.

Why you need it

The sale of products and/or services is the primary method of developing revenue. Any reader of a plan is going to have a key interest in the level of revenue now and future expectation. It explains what the source of revenue is and indicates the strategy that will be used to maintain or grow those revenues.

Products and services: level 1

EXISTING PRODUCTS AND SERVICES

Without getting into too much detail, explain the range. If there are only four or five products they can be listed, but if there are more you can include the product list in an appendix if you wish.

Benefits

Focus on the benefits your customers get from buying your products or services. Don't mix benefits up with features. A feature is a technical aspect of the product or service which should result in a benefit to the customer.

Example

You may be selling a television which has a remote control. The remote control is a *feature*; the *benefit* it delivers is that the customer doesn't have to get up and walk across the room to change channels.

It generally costs money to add features to products so they really need to pay their way. If the benefit delivered to the customer is not worth what it costs to include it, the product will probably sell better without the feature at a lower price.

Showing that you understand the importance of delivering benefits to customers is an indication of being customer focused, and that is likely to help the reader feel more confident about the business.

USPs (unique selling points)

The most important benefits are the ones you deliver that your competitors can't. They provide excellent reasons why customers should buy from you rather than from competitors. Work out what they are and, while you are at it, try to think of new ones you could introduce. The most important point to remember is that if the customer doesn't value it, the USP is useless.

INTRODUCING NEW PRODUCTS AND SERVICES

Explain your rationale

This is your reason for introducing the product. It may be something that existing customers are already buying elsewhere, or something which would be easy to introduce as it uses capabilities you already have.

Evaluate the market opportunity

What makes you feel there is a market for what you propose? If your typical customers have told you they are buying x of these a month, put it in the plan. If your customers have told you they are not happy with their current suppliers because of A, B and C, write it down. You may have got the idea from reading an article in a trade journal or a newspaper. It may be that a competitor has introduced the product and is doing well with it. The more evidence you have the better. Evidence is far more important than mere hearsay.

Why us?

Explain why you are qualified to exploit this opportunity. Focus on the skills you have in your team, the capability and the capacity you have available. Any new product which uses up currently unused capacity is especially valuable. (Figure 7.1 gives a level-1 products plan builder.)

Existing products/services
Range
Benefits
USPs
New products
Rationale
Market opportunity
Why us?

Figure 7.1   Products plan builder, level 1

TOP TIP

Always look at your products and services from your customers' point of view.

Products and services: level 2

Carry out the processes covered in level 1 and then move on to the following. Don't use the level-1 business plan builder as the one in this section covers everything.

Existing products and services

Range

Describe the range of products and, if possible, explain which groups of customers (see Chapter 4) are buying which products. It may be helpful to fill in the matrix shown in Figure 7.2.

Customer groups	Products											
	1	2	3	4	5	6	7	8	9	10	11	12
A	✓		✓		✓	✓	✓		✓			✓
B				✓			✓		✓			
C	✓	✓	✓						✓	✓	✓	
D			✓	✓	✓		✓					
E	✓	✓	✓	✓	✓	✓	✓	✓	✓	✓	✓	✓

Figure 7.2   Product matrix worksheet

This exercise can show up groups that are not buying a particular product which they are clearly using. The next step is obviously to ask yourself: why? It may be that an individual salesperson needs additional training or that there is need for a marketing campaign.

Winners and losers

Some products will undoubtedly be more successful than others. You can grade them on sales, quality and profit:

■ *Sales:* you can expect 80% of your sales to come from just 20% of your products. Do you know which the 20% are, and do you know why?

■ *Quality:* some products are more reliable than others. Which are the products that prove most troublesome and why is this? If the troublesome ones are big sellers, remedial action should probably be a priority if possible.

■ *Profit:* you can also expect 80% of your profits to come from 20% of your products. This is not necessarily the same 20% that generates 80% of your sales. Do you know which products they are and why that is so?

Gaps

From the above analysis it may be evident that there are gaps. Products that would fit nicely into the range but aren't there yet. What do you think they are?

New products and services

Market opportunity

You need to show some evidence of market research that demonstrates a demand for the proposed offering.

Primary market research: collect information from both your existing customers and prospective customers. This can be done when you happen to be in contact with a customer anyway.

Everyone in the business who has direct contact with customers should be involved in this exercise. This includes both salespeople and technicians. Keep a record of what the various people have said and refer to it in the plan. There is no need to go into too much detail. Remember the plan may get into the hands of competitors!

Secondary market research: this is published research which someone else has already done. The Internet is usually the first port of call. Market reports are published by organisations such as Keynote (www.keynote.co.uk) and Mintel (www.mintel.com). They are very useful, especially for forecasting the future performance of a market. There are shortcomings, however:

- There may not be a report for your market.
- The market covered may be too wide for you.
- The geographical area of the report may be inappropriate.
- The report could be out of date.
- The report may be expensive.

Some public libraries hold copies of certain reports. They may also be able to borrow a copy from another library for you to inspect. (Figure 7.3 gives a level-2 products plan builder.)

Existing products
Range
Benefits
USPs
Winners and losers
Gaps
New products
Rationale
Market opportunity
Why us?

Figure 7.3   Products plan builder, level 2

Products and services: level 3

Most of the topics have been covered at levels 1 and 2. We will now look at some new ones.

PRODUCT PORTFOLIO

Product lifecycle

All products have a lifecycle which starts at introduction and ends with decline and finally withdrawal (see Figure 7.4).

If a new product is introduced successfully, repeat purchases increase and more customers eventually get to hear about it. Sales grow very quickly for a time, during which period new competitors often enter the market which is further expanded by their marketing efforts. The rate of growth slows as the product enters the maturity stage. A point is reached where there are too many competitors in the market. This leads to falling margins with some firms dropping out. Finally the market moves into decline as customers possibly find better solutions.

The profit produced follows a different path from the sales (see Figure 7.5). It can be seen that in its early stages the typical product creates a significant

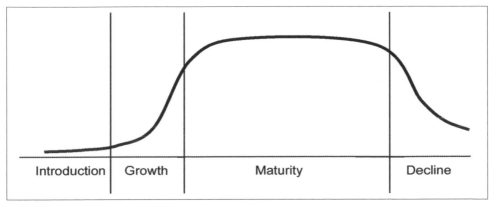

Figure 7.4   Product lifecycle

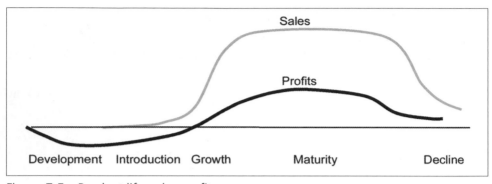

Figure 7.5   Product lifecycle: profit

drain on resources. Generally, profits actually peak at the early part of maturity, after which the new competitors force margins down.

Portfolio management

The principle of portfolio management is that by having a number of products at various stages of the product lifecycle curve, the business will have the ideal balance between current and future profits. The highly profitable mature products can fund the products under development and those in the introductory stage.

From the research you carried out on your products' market, attempt to place each of them on the curve. You should have a nice spread of products in each of the sections of the curve. If you have too many in the development and introduction stages and not enough that are mature, you almost definitely have cash-flow problems. If all the products are mature or declining, profits will be good but future prospects poor.

Explain your portfolio in terms of how many products are at each stage of the cycle and how planned new product introduction will impact on this. (Figure 7.6 gives a level-3 products plan builder.)

Existing products
Range
Benefits
USPs
Winners and losers
Gaps
Product portfolio
New products
Rationale
Market opportunity
Why us?

Figure 7.6   Products plan builder, level 3

8

Determining critical success factors

Your critical success factors (CSFs) are the four or five things you have to get right to succeed in the business you are in. They are the elements that are vital if you are going to implement your strategy successfully. Excellence in CSFs will give you the golden edge.

Critical success factors are different for different organisations and are chiefly determined by the type of business you are in and the markets you are serving. Some of them are common to all businesses, however.

Why you need it

You don't just need it, you can't do without it. These are the small number of factors that are mostly responsible for separating the winners from the losers. Just think about it. These are the things which are probably the difference between being a roaring success and an abject failure. Skip this one at your peril.

CSF: level 1

Digging for gold

Discovering your CSFs is the vital first stage. Remember there are only four or five of them and they are things that you have to get right.

It's a good idea to get your team together and brainstorm the question. Make sure you include the salespeople.

What are the five things that matter most in the business you are in?

Get ideas, create a big list and then whittle it down.

You should also ask your customers what they feel is most important. You should already have done that, of course, because if you don't know what your customer actually values, you are lacking that all important customer focus. Refer to the customer needs worksheet (Chapter 4).

> ## TOP TIP
>
> Don't assume you know what the customers value, ask them!

DISCOVERING CSFS

CSFs could be lurking anywhere in your business. Try carrying out a PRIMOF exercise. This identifies sections of the organisation where they are likely to reside:

- **People:** have people with the required skills and attitude.
- **Resources:** equipment, facilities, and funding to succeed.
- **Innovation:** implementing enough new ideas.
- **Marketing:** giving customers what they want. Customer satisfaction levels.

CSF possibilities		
Section	CSF	Importance out of 10
People Resources Innovation Marketing Operations Finance		

Figure 8.1   CSF worksheet

- **Operations:** consistent quality. On-time delivery. Being the lowest-cost supplier.
- **Finance:** cash flow. Profitability.

These are broad examples that can be refined as desired. (Figure 8.1 gives a CSF worksheet.)

COMPETITORS

Some competitors are clearly more successful than others. Try to work out what it is about the successful ones that separates them from the rest.

IMPROVING CSF STRATEGY

Now you've got your four or five critical success factors it's time to think about how you can improve them.

Rate each CSF that you have identified out of 10 depending on how important it is to the success of your business, in regard to productivity or customer appeal. The more important they are, the bigger an impact any improvement will have.

For each one, think about what you can do in the coming year to improve your position in it. Try to set yourself specific, measurable goals. Set a date in your diary for when you will monitor CSF progress. (Figure 8.2 gives a level-1 CSF plan builder.)

CSFs
1.
2.
3.
4.
5.
CSF improvement plan
1.
2.
3.
4.
5.

Figure 8.2   CSF plan builder, level 1

TOP TIP

Build your strategy on CSFs.

CSF: level 2

Scoring yourself

In level 1 you have established and rated about five critical success factors.

Now you need to move on and score your current performance out of 10 for each CSF. If the CSF relates to an internal efficiency issue, ask yourself how you compare with perfection. Perfection is 10. Look at how other companies are performing in that area. You may set up an agreement with a similar type of business, which doesn't compete with you, to help each other improve.

If there is a customer-facing issue, you should use customer feedback to determine how you are performing. A good customer satisfaction system, which elicits feedback, can be very rewarding in itself.

Now use the importance of each CSF to calculate weighting. The weights must add up to 10 and reflect the importance of each.

Next, multiply your current performance by the weighting to come up with your overall score for each CSF. Then add up your overall scores to get your current CSF rating.

Example

CSF	Weighting	Current performance	Overall score
Reliability of product	5	4	20
Aftersales service	2	6	12
On-time delivery	1	5	5
Price	2	5	10
Current CSF rating			47%

This rating is very important. It shows your overall current performance in relation to Critical Success Factors. As these are the crucial determiners of success, seriously to win in your market you need to get pretty close to 100%.

Looking at the above example, it can be seen that the easiest way of boosting the rating is to improve in the area of highest importance. In this example it is increasing the reliability of the product. Increasing product reliability from 4 to 7 would increase the overall rating to 62%. That has the potential to put a lot of profit in your pocket. (Figure 8.3 gives a level-2 CSF plan builder.)

CSFs	Weighting	Current performance	Overall score
1. 2. 3. 4. 5.			
Current CSF rating			
Improvement priorities			

Figure 8.3   CSF plan builder: level 2

TOP TIP
Complete level 1 before tackling level 2.

CSF: level 3

Complete the previous level before starting this section.

COMPARE THE MARKET

Having established in level 2 your current CSF ratings, it would now be a good idea to compare yourself with your major competitors. Carry out the exercise in level 2 for each of your main competitors. If there are more than three highly significant ones, start with the three most important.

This exercise will use intelligence on your *competitors* gathered over time (Chapter 5).

This exercise, properly carried out, will show you what you are up against. The results can be used in the development of your SWOT (Chapter 9) and in the formation of your strategic plans (Chapter 11). (Figure 8.4 gives a level-3 CSF plan builder.)

CSFs	Current performance				Weighting	Scores (performance × weighting)			
	You	Comp A	Comp B	Comp C	Score	You	Comp A	Comp B	Comp C
1.									
2.									
3.									
4.									
5.									
Current CSF rating						%	%	%	%
Improvement priorities									

Figure 8.4   CSF plan builder, level 3

9

SWOTing your competitors

The SWOT is probably the most used and abused tool in business planning. There is a very common scenario. Having been asked to prepare a SWOT someone makes:

- a list of Strengths,
- a list of Weaknesses,
- a list of Opportunities and
- a list of Threats.

That accomplished, they briefly admire their handiwork, and then get on with something else, giving the SWOT no further thought. Unfortunately the whole exercise has been a pointless waste of time.

Why you need it

Done properly, however, it can help you differentiate yourself from competitors. It can point you in the right direction to make changes that will help you win more profitable business from your competitors.

Your SWOT: level 1

Your SWOT is a great way of summarising a lot of the information you have gathered when you carried out your research (see Figure 9.1).

SWOT stands for Strengths, Weaknesses, Opportunities and Threats. It is normally presented as a simple matrix that outlines the main issues. It is important that you think on the macro level and not get involved with details. You are concerned with the issues only.

THE BASIC SWOT MATRIX

Strengths and weaknesses (see Figure 9.2) relate to the here and now. This is reality. Opportunities and threats relate to the future. They may or may not materialise. Carrying out this exercise with rose-coloured glasses in place is frequently done, but will not help. Say it like it is and then use the tool to make it better.

You may be selling a range of product groups to a selection of markets. The issues involved with this will be dealt with in detail in level 3. For now you can concentrate on your major product group and your major market. This will probably account for well over half your business, so it is a great start point.

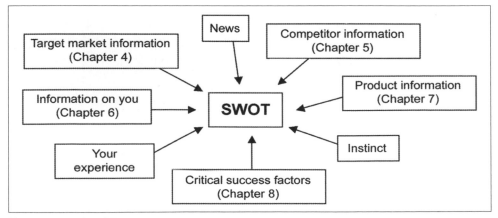

Figure 9.1   SWOT

Strengths	Weaknesses
Opportunities	Threats

Figure 9.2 Basic SWOT matrix

STRENGTHS AND WEAKNESSES

The first question we have to address is: 'What exactly is a strength?' Most people probably think, quite wrongly, that the answer is: 'something we are pretty good at.'

A strength is something you do better than your competitors.

Example

Let's imagine you sell ice cream. Your customers were asked to rate your product and they said:

Evaluation of ice cream	7/10
Evaluation of cone	4/10

On the basis of that you may, quite reasonably, say that your ice-cream quality is a strength and your cone quality is a weakness.

The customers were then asked to evaluate the offerings of your three main competitors and the average result was:

Evaluation of ice cream	9/10
Evaluation of cone	2/10

It can now be seen that the quality of your ice cream is in fact a weakness and the quality of your cone is a strength.

Gather all the information and list your main strengths. Then ask yourself how important each is, giving it a mark out of 10. If you are not sure what is important, ask your customers!

If you do something equally as well as, or equally as badly as, your competitors, it is neither a strength nor a weakness. If you are all doing badly with it, and customers think it is important, then improving in that aspect could represent a major opportunity. Likewise, a competitor improving when you didn't would represent a threat.

OPPORTUNITIES AND THREATS

This is where you need to get your antennae out and anticipate what may or may not happen in the future.

Whereas strengths and weaknesses are applied exclusively to you, opportunities and threats affect everyone in the marketplace.

Some opportunities have the potential to transform your business absolutely into something much bigger and better, while some threats have the potential of being catastrophic. Enter the key opportunities and threats into the matrix and rate each one out of 10 for potential impact on your business. A 10-rated threat can easily put you out of business so it demands attention.

Before you get too despondent, you must remember that the whole thing about opportunities and threats is they may not happen at all!

Go through your opportunities and threats and rate out of 10 what you think the chances are that they will actually happen.

For each opportunity and threat there is now an impact rating and a probability rating. Multiply them together to arrive at the *significance* (out of 100). Clearly the higher the number, the more essential it is to plan an action to strengthen your position in regard to it. Numbers don't have to be very high to be important. A threat with a score of 10 on impact and 5 on likelihood only scores 50 overall, but there is a 50% chance it could put you out of business.

Now take a few paragraphs to explain the significance of the SWOT on the business, focusing on the key issues (see Figure 9.3). Explain which ones you will be prioritising action on.

Strengths			Importance	Weaknesses			Importance
Opportunities	Impact	Likelihood	Significance	**Threats**	Impact	Likelihood	Significance
Conclusion							

Figure 9.3 SWOT plan builder, level 1

TOP TIP

When something unexpected happens, the player who has best prepared for it sees an improvement in competitive advantage.

Your SWOT: level 2

What has been covered at level 1 still applies here, but we are now going to try to make it more strategic.

MAKING SWOT MORE STRATEGIC

Strengths

These are things you do better than competitors and the key strategy here is *leverage*. Have you made sure that all your customers and potential customers are aware of their existence? Can you think of programmes to communicate them better? This obviously applies especially to the ones that customers rate as most important.

Weaknesses

Some weaknesses are not important to customers, or to our internal efficiency, while others are seriously holding us back. A good strategy here would be prioritised neutralisation. This is more pragmatic than trying to turn weaknesses into strengths. Ultimately, however, after neutralisation, if it is important to the customer, strategies can be developed to turn them into strengths.

Opportunities

You will invariably be better positioned to take advantage of some opportunities than others. An appropriate strategy would involve repositioning to capitalise better. It is important to prioritise those opportunities with high *potential impact* (see level 1).

Threats

An appropriate strategy is to prepare a *defence* against threats. Clearly the emphasis should be placed on those with the highest *potential impact*.

SWOT strategy matrix

A little tool that some people find helpful in developing these strategies presents the SWOT in a different way (see Figure 9.4).

	Strengths	Weaknesses
Opportunities	SO issues	WO issues
Threats	ST issues	WT issues

Figure 9.4   SWOT strategy matrix worksheet

SO issues

These are opportunities that show overall alignment to your strengths. You are naturally in a position to gain more from them than your competitors are. If they are viable, these are opportunities that you would probably choose to take advantage of and look at what needs to be done in preparation. Investment in these areas is likely to provide a healthy return.

WO issues

These are opportunities that require the overcoming of weaknesses to capitalise on. For those that offer sufficient potential, a strategy will need to be developed. Attractive returns on investment are possible if your capability makes them viable.

ST issues

Develop strategies that use your strengths to reduce your vulnerability and risk. These threats are generally fairly easy to defend against, with subsequent investment being safe and probably necessary. When prioritising, take account of the significance rating.

WT issues

Significance is again very important. The business is likely to be seriously exposed to this threat and a defensive plan may well be urgently needed.

Use this additional analysis to develop better strategic input in the conclusions section of the plan builder. Express your conclusions as possible strategies. These possible strategies will then be evaluated during the strategic planning section of the process (Chapter 11).

In your plan this will demonstrate a good understanding of the risks and will outline your approach to alleviating them.

TOP TIP

The SWOT offers an ideal opportunity to summarise what you have discovered in your research so far.

Use the business plan builder from level 1.

Your SWOT: level 3

This section offers a refinement of level 1. Level 2 is still applicable.

MULTITUDINOUS SWOTS

In level 1 a single SWOT was carried out, focused on the major product/ market groups. Most businesses have more than one group of products aimed at more than one market. It is likely that different conditions exist for the different groupings and what will ultimately be needed is a strategy for each.

Example

A company may be manufacturing a range of domestic sewing machines which are sold to the general public via electrical retailers, and a range of industrial sewing machines which are sold direct to the factories that use them. Even though the products are fundamentally the same, a totally different strategy would be needed for each and the two SWOTs would look very different.

Grouping products and markets

Experience and common sense will tell you which products go together to form a product group. If you made three different sewing machines with different features aimed at different price points in the same market you would clearly have one group. If you also had a food mixer aimed at the same group of customers and distributed in the same way, it would form a different product group and would need a separate SWOT.

If the food mixer was being sold in the UK and in France, two SWOTs would be needed even though the product is exactly the same.

A single market segment is a group of buyers with similar major characteristics, i.e. they have a shared need which we can plan to satisfy.

Where do you draw the line?

Too many SWOTs can get confusing, while too few can be too generalised and meaningless. A reasonable start point would be to pick your five or six major product/market groups and prepare a separate SWOT for each. You can then develop five or six strategies to overcome competitors.

Preparing six SWOTs is not six times the work of preparing one. There will be a lot of commonality. Even if one SWOT is 90% the same as another, the 10% of it which is different can be the key to winning in the market.

Clearly, to go back to our example of the industrial and domestic sewing machines, a single strategy covering both would be ludicrous. The whole point of a SWOT is that it becomes a natural spawning ground for powerful strategies that strengthen the firm's competitive position and drive profits higher. Strategies flow from a well conceived SWOT. Your SWOT becomes the ideal start point for what is covered in Chapter 11 (strategy).

The level-1 business plan builder can again be used, but when you write this part of the plan be sure to explain the conclusions SWOT by SWOT strategically. In other words, you will be outlining very broadly the approaches that could be taken to deal with the issues. This will give the reader the confidence of knowing that you understand the business battlefields you operate in.

10

Developing your vision

DARE TO DREAM

Good business leaders are never satisfied; and that's what makes them good business leaders.

Anyone who starts a business is a visionary. When you started your business, you pictured in your mind what it was going to look like and how you wanted it to develop.

As the years go by and more and more people join, the vision tends to get polluted by events and the views of others. Without consciously revisiting it, you are likely to reach a point where you don't even know what the vision is any more. Worse still, it may mean different things to different people.

It's time to get everyone pointing in the same direction; to do again what was done when you started the business. Visualise where it's headed, and communicate that throughout your team so everyone can start singing from the same hymn sheet.

This is the most luxurious part of planning; there are no shackles and you have the opportunity to imagine how your business will be in the future. How exactly you would like it to be if you were able to choose. This is your chance to describe your ideal future, without having to worry about how to actually create it. Your vision will subsequently be crystallised into a *mission statement* which will appear as part of the *company description*.

Why you need it

Once you have a vision of what you want the business to become and you convey that to the people who matter, everyone knows the destination. If there isn't a commonly agreed destination you lose the guiding light. You need to understand where you are now, and where you want to get to. Without this, the business lacks direction and underperforms.

Investors will also pay particular attention to this part of the plan. They like to back visionaries, and like to back firms which are expected to grow. A growing business is likely to give them a higher return than a stagnant one. It should also give the owners a higher return.

Your vision: level 1

PURPOSE

Apart from making a profit and earning a living for the people working in them, all businesses have a fundamental purpose. In each case, it's the reason for the existence of the business. It is the way a business makes its profits. It is an often idealistic reason for being. It is a guiding light to your team. It is a big determiner of what you do and how you do it (see Figure 10.1).

Example

Disney's stated purpose is *to make people happy* and that actually controls everything they do in their business.

Example

GM's stated vision: *our vision is to be the world's leader in transportation products and related services.* As a conglomerate, the underlying purpose is to assemble a group of strategic business units in that sector that are world leaders. To back that up they have a strategy of ensuring that every business they own can only be No.1

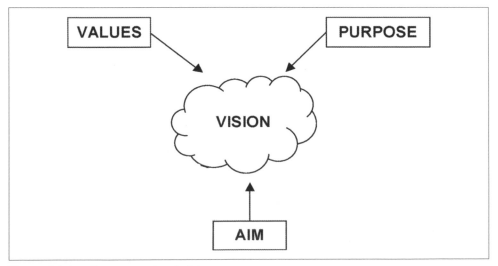

Figure 10.1   Components of vision

or No.2 in its market. If they are unconvinced that it can achieve that they dispose of it. This is a perfect example of vision determining actions. If their vision had been *We want to beat Ford* their actions would have been completely different.

Example

Tesco's stated purpose is: *to create value for customers to earn their lifetime loyalty.* That vision was a key factor in their becoming No.1.

Try to focus on where you are trying to position yourself in the market and avoid making your purpose product orientated. Focus on what customer group you are targeting or what you want to achieve.

Let's assume you are selling central heating systems. Your first stab at purpose may be to say:

We sell central heating systems.

You then need to take it a stage further:

We help people keep their properties warm for the lowest possible initial outlay.

or:

We sell the very best heating systems.

or:

We help people who want to keep their homes warm and save fuel by having the most efficient system possible.

or:

We sell the best looking heating systems.

You could now take it a stage further by adding a location:

We sell the very best heating systems to families living in Somerset.

Clearly, the way you and your team will now behave depends on which option you have chosen.

VALUES

Your values are the timeless guiding principles that govern the way you run your business. You only need to think of five or six, but they do need to be core values. These values should form an unchanging bedrock that will probably still be there in 20 years' time.

Don't just make a list of things that sound good. List the genuine values that the business operates around. These are the values that your business will honour – every time. They should provide guidance to a member of your team who has to make a decision. If you are fed up with people continually asking you what should be done about this and that, give them the list of values to use as a guide to making decisions themselves. The list won't enable people to make good decisions *per se*, but it will give them a framework that will make the solution to many problems obvious. Be very careful when you draw up your values list because you are saying to all your people that this is how you want them to behave.

If you want to see some examples of values, have a look at the values checklist in level 2. Remember the values you are choosing are those that are currently there. We need to be clear what our values are before we start looking at strategy.

AIM

How would you like your business to look in five or even ten years' time? Is your vision that it will be twice the size, five times the size, ten times the size? Will you be working where you are working now or going further afield? Will you be selling what you are selling now, or will it be completely different?

You don't really have to concern yourself too much with reality and you don't even have to give any thought to how you will get there (that's covered in the strategy section). As long as you believe your vision is possible, it's fine. Just be visionary. (Figure 10.2 gives a level-1 mission plan builder.)

Mission statement
Purpose
Values
Aim

Figure 10.2   Mission plan builder, level 1

TOP TIP

Think big when you decide what your aim is. Don't let reality restrict you. The aim doesn't have to look feasible at this stage, but don't write down the impossible. If you believe it's possible, it's fine. If you are turning over £100,000 now, an aim to turn over £10 billion in five years would be ludicrous, but to aim at £5 million sounds reasonable to me.

Your vision: level 2

Refer to level 1 and then refine it.

Purpose

At level 1 we looked at clarifying the reason to exist. When your business was originally started the owners will have had a vision of how they were going to do things. That viewpoint may have evolved over the years, but there will still be a clear modus operandi.

The owners, however, are probably not the only people working in the business. The objective here is to:

1. Find out what other people in the business believe the purpose to be;
2. Discuss the merits of other views;
3. Consider adapting the original purpose; and
4. Communicate the purpose to everyone in the business.

Step 1 can be a real eye opener. The owners of the business, or senior managers, are usually not the ones who have most contact with customers. This can result in a high degree of incongruence within the organisation, leading to mixed messages.

It is very interesting to get the viewpoints of various people in the business as to what they believe the current purpose is, and what they believe it should be. Ultimately it is for senior management to decide what the purpose actually is, but ideas from the workforce can enrich that, and even if it doesn't, people are more likely wholeheartedly to buy into the stated purpose if they feel they have been consulted.

Remember, purpose should determine the behaviour of each and every person working in the business. So each and every person should know what it is. If it is not communicated, the sense of purpose is lost.

Be very cautious when considering adapting purpose as it should be enduring and embedded into the culture. It would most definitely not be changed year by year when the annual planning is done. Only adapt it if the original has become out of date and is incongruous with the current aims.

Values

As individuals we all have our set of values by which we run our lives. Our own personal set of values is fairly unique to us, but we tend to feel most comfortable with people who have similar value sets. They could be described as the broad preferences by which we live our lives; that determine our sense of what is right and wrong. These values influence our attitudes and the way we behave. What is abhorrent to one person is a totally acceptable way of behaving to another. Confliction of value sets is probably a major reason for the breakdown of personal relationships.

Similarly each business has its own value set and these have probably developed over time. They have undoubtedly been influenced by the personal value sets of the individuals working in the business. An individual whose personal value set differs greatly from that of the organisation will probably feel uncomfortable working in that environment. So when you are recruiting, try to find people whose values are not dissimilar to those of the business. We can all cite instances of new recruits 'just not fitting in'.

What we are trying to do here is discover what the values in the business actually are at the moment. You may try giving a wide range of people working in the business the checklist given in Figure 10.3 for them to complete. Add a few extras of your own and take off those you don't think apply or just create your own list.

Analysis of values checklist

Everyone will have rated each of the values for how it actually is from 0 to 10. Average the score for each value. Just add the scores given for each value and divide by the number of forms returned.

The values that have scored around 9 or 10 are probably your core values. There shouldn't be more than 5 or 6. If a higher number scored 9 or 10 discuss as a team which are really the core values.

Aim

As level 1. Use the level-1 business plan builder.

Please rate how important each of the following values actually are in the business as a whole now. This is not how important you personally feel each one should be but how it is in the business now. If you feel that it really is a core value, rate it 10. If you feel that it is not an issue in the business, rate it 0. Please be truthful.

Value		Low										High
		0	1	2	3	4	5	6	7	8	9	10
Customer delight	Not just satisfaction	☐	☐	☐	☐	☐	☐	☐	☐	☐	☐	☐
Continuous improvement	Every day in every way	☐	☐	☐	☐	☐	☐	☐	☐	☐	☐	☐
Creativity	Finding better ways of doing things	☐	☐	☐	☐	☐	☐	☐	☐	☐	☐	☐
Honesty	Truthfulness with ourselves and others	☐	☐	☐	☐	☐	☐	☐	☐	☐	☐	☐
People development	Improvement of capability	☐	☐	☐	☐	☐	☐	☐	☐	☐	☐	☐
No blame culture	We learn from our mistakes and move on	☐	☐	☐	☐	☐	☐	☐	☐	☐	☐	☐
Communication	Telling what's going on	☐	☐	☐	☐	☐	☐	☐	☐	☐	☐	☐
Teamwork	All pulling together	☐	☐	☐	☐	☐	☐	☐	☐	☐	☐	☐
Discipline	Adherence to rules	☐	☐	☐	☐	☐	☐	☐	☐	☐	☐	☐
Accountability	For performance, results, problems	☐	☐	☐	☐	☐	☐	☐	☐	☐	☐	☐
Empowerment	Giving individuals the authority to solve problems	☐	☐	☐	☐	☐	☐	☐	☐	☐	☐	☐
Standardisation	Set procedures	☐	☐	☐	☐	☐	☐	☐	☐	☐	☐	☐
Integrity	Doing what we say	☐	☐	☐	☐	☐	☐	☐	☐	☐	☐	☐
Respect	Treating others as we would like to be treated	☐	☐	☐	☐	☐	☐	☐	☐	☐	☐	☐
Community	Being a force for good	☐	☐	☐	☐	☐	☐	☐	☐	☐	☐	☐
Winning	We aim to come first	☐	☐	☐	☐	☐	☐	☐	☐	☐	☐	☐
Quality	Of products and services	☐	☐	☐	☐	☐	☐	☐	☐	☐	☐	☐
Reliability	We constantly perform	☐	☐	☐	☐	☐	☐	☐	☐	☐	☐	☐
Responsiveness	We react quickly	☐	☐	☐	☐	☐	☐	☐	☐	☐	☐	☐
Safety	Of everyone we deal with	☐	☐	☐	☐	☐	☐	☐	☐	☐	☐	☐
Fun	We enjoy ourselves in work	☐	☐	☐	☐	☐	☐	☐	☐	☐	☐	☐

Figure 10.3   Values checklist

Your vision: level 3

Purpose
As Level 2

Values
In level 2 you determined what the five or six core values are at the moment. As a team how do you feel about that? The probability is that no one ever sat down and decided what the values were to be. They often simply evolve over time, with the development of the culture of the business.

Changing the values would be a difficult and dangerous exercise because we are dealing with deeply held cultural beliefs that reflect the personal cultures of the team.

It is still worth asking yourself what you would like the values actually to be. Involve as many people as you can in this exercise. Don't try to change too much or move too quickly. Remember this is just a vision. We are trying to establish guidance that may be used in our strategic planning. Don't create action plans now, just try to agree how you would like to see it evolve. If the team agrees and you set it out in your vision, which is well communicated, in time you should start to move towards it, without actually doing anything. The key point is that the new value mix remains in principle compatible with the personal value sets of the team. So you wouldn't normally try to move too far.

Include the shift in values in the aims section of the vision. This subtle shift in values will certainly be a very real aim.

Aim
Isn't it time you created a monster?

What you really need is a monster goal. It's big, it's audacious, and it's a little bit frightening. It's something you are aiming for in the distant future.

Sit down with your team and agree on what your monster goal should be. It's not going to happen soon, we are probably talking about 10 or 20 years in the future. Don't worry about being realistic – if you believe it's possible, it's ok. Don't worry about how you are going to achieve it – just achieve it.

A monster goal is a beacon to head towards. Even though it may be impossible to achieve it for a long time it can still be your guiding light.

It has to be big enough and important enough to excite and maybe terrify your team.

Example

Back in the 1950s, Japanese products had a laughable reputation. When children received a present, they would carefully inspect it looking for the dreaded 'made in Japan' inscription. On finding it they would know that there was little point in getting too attached to it, because it would soon be broken.

At the time, manufacturing costs were very low in Japan, and the goods were very cheap and nasty.

Against this backdrop, Sony set themselves a monster goal in 1954:

Our goal is to become the company most known for changing the worldwide image of Japanese products as being of poor quality.

Use the level-1 plan builder.

11

Choosing your business strategy

Strategy formation is probably the most important part of the business planning process. The chosen *business strategy* should describe how the organisation will move towards its vision by succeeding in the marketplace against its competitors. A business does this through competitive advantage and the strategy should aim to strengthen that.

It should be focused on meeting customer needs better than competitors do, through leveraging the distinctive competencies of the business. If you can do the things your customer values most highly, better than your competitors, you will have a strong competitive advantage. Resultantly, you will gain a better understanding of where you should concentrate your efforts to improve.

Corporate strategy comes before *business strategy*, but it only applies to a large conglomerate which owns many businesses. It deals with the policy of managing the group businesses and establishing the types of businesses that should be started, acquired or sold. Having determined corporate strategy, a separate business strategy is formulated for each group member.

Why you need it

Choosing the correct strategy or not will directly control the amount of profit you make. Over the years the right strategy can make you millions, while the wrong strategy can cost you millions.

The right strategy, well communicated, can give you a happy, contented team, all pulling together in the right direction. The wrong strategy can easily lead to discontent, unrest and a stressed-out team.

If you are looking for finance, your reader will pay particular attention to your strategy. It is a very real indicator of the organisation's likelihood of success.

Business strategy: level 1

Strategy is the way in which you plan to achieve your aims. You will need to use the hard data which have been gathered along the way and crystallised in the strategy plan builder (Figure 11.2), but don't underestimate the value of *soft data*.

Many highly effective managers and leaders place a lot more emphasis on soft data than hard data. Soft data come from observations, casual discussions and even gossip. They rely heavily on gut feelings, intuition and experience. Some people are so good at ferreting out and interpreting soft data that they have no real need for hard data at all. For most of us, we need both.

Whichever way you do it, however, ultimately, when everything is weighed up and finely balanced, a strategy has to be chosen. Unfortunately, you invariably have to work with incomplete information.

SURVIVING THE BUSINESS BATTLEFIELD

Customers have a choice to make. They will either buy from you or a competitor (Figure 11.1). Which competitor is irrelevant because, if a sale is lost, it is lost.

Successfully adapting your business strategy, through the understanding of customer needs and competitor offerings, will result in some customers who previously would have gone to the competition coming to you.

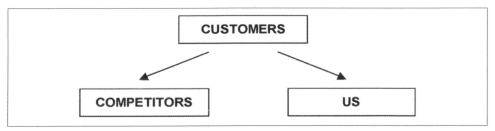

Figure 11.1   The business battlefield

You need to discover what can be done differently to attract these new customers while holding on to the ones you already have.

FINDING IDEAS

Top down

Ideas don't generally come on demand. They sometimes pop into your head when you are least expecting it. When they do, write them down. It would also be worth encouraging the rest of your team to do the same.

In a strategic meeting with your top team, try brainstorming new ideas. Start by focusing on the vision (Chapter 10) and try to think up things that could be done to take you there.

Bottom up

Communicate the vision throughout the workforce and actively encourage everybody to make suggestions. Some of the best ideas come from people 'at the coal face'.

Evaluating ideas

Most ideas will probably be very quickly rejected, some will fall into the 'why didn't we think of that before' category, while some may need some thinking about. Choose the ones you want to run with and incorporate them into your business strategy, along with what you are going to continue doing.

Example

Virgin Trains Vision: *To become the most safe, consistent, reliable and profitable of the train operating franchises in a climate that respects different views, where people need not be afraid to be open and honest.*

- It sets out key business values.
- It indicates commercial aims.
- It indicates the relationship between the organisation and its people.

Purpose: *To satisfy customers so they use the service over and over.*

Strategy: *To encourage the interaction of front line employees with customers. The reason is to improve the customers' overall experience and discover ways of improving performance.*

Managers are expected to encourage this behaviour and actively seek suggestions from workers on how to improve the operation.

STRATEGIC INTENT

Describe generally how you intend to change the business in the future. This should be a brief crystallisation of the vision (Chapter 10). It is a statement of what you intend to achieve rather than how it will be done. This is the natural start point of your strategy development. It can also encompass any opportunities that you have identified and would like to take advantage of (Chapter 9).

CRITICAL SUCCESS FACTORS

Chapter 8.

CUSTOMER NEEDS

Customer needs worksheet (Chapter 4: target market).

DISTINCTIVE COMPETENCIES

Chapter 9 (strengths).

STRATEGY STATEMENT

Outline what you now intend to do differently to achieve your aims.

RISK FACTORS

These are the things that could go wrong, and an indication of what you will do if that is the case. The fact that you have a contingency plan will give lenders a lot more confidence (Chapter 9: weaknesses and threats). Figure 11.2 gives a level-1 strategy plan builder.

Business strategy
Strategic intent
Critical success factors
Customer needs
Distinctive competencies
Strategy statement
Risk factors

Figure 11.2   Strategy plan builder, level 1

TOP TIP

Don't try to get too much detail in your strategy: that comes in the operational plans (Chapters 13–16).

Business strategy: level 2

Work through level 1 first and then use the following to refine your strategy.

FUNDAMENTAL BUSINESS STRATEGIES

Figure 11.3 summarizes the fundamental business strategies.

Cost

Being the lowest-cost producer is a great position to be in. Total costs are lower than they are for all your competitors.

If you really have got a lower cost base than your competitors, you could follow a low-price strategy. In a price war the supplier with the lowest cost base is the likely winner. This is not necessarily a good idea as you can end up with wafer-thin margins which may put your business at risk.

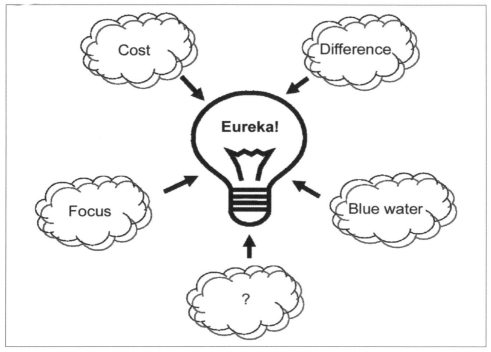

Figure 11.3   Fundamental strategies

Also beware of the fact that if you are competing locally with a large national organisation, they can cut prices and operate at a temporary loss in your area, until you are driven out of business.

Likewise, you can be a national player, but if your competitor is part of a conglomerate, they can run that business at a loss in an attempt to drive you out of the market.

Undercutting competitors is an aggressive strategy which is likely to draw a response.

Used with finesse, the position of lowest-cost supplier is a very, very powerful one. Even if you are in this hallowed position, it would still be better not to compete on price alone.

Difference

Differentiation involves creating uniqueness in your product or service. There are many different ways in which that can be done.

Examples

Brand	*Mercedes cars*
Dealer network	*Caterpillar*
Technology	*Apple*
Reliability	*Panasonic*
Style	*Gucci*

This differentiation should be something customers value and be prepared to pay a premium for. With a successful differentiation strategy you don't have to compete on price.

Just imagine the power of having both differentiation and being the lowest-cost supplier. In that instance, high margins can potentially be generated.

Focus

Focus is about concentration. By concentrating on just one buyer group, a very narrow product range or a very small geographic market, a firm is able to adapt its offering to the specific needs of that group far better than could a competitor who was not specialising.

Focus is a form of differentiation, in that the offer is specifically tailored to the needs of the group it is serving. Because it's only serving one group, efficiency is higher and costs lower. Focus is a powerful strategy but it doesn't lend itself to enabling high market share for obvious reasons. A focused firm can, however, be highly profitable.

Example
Saga Holidays sell package holidays exclusively to the over 50s.

Blue water
One way of winning is to stop competing.

Why go where all the competitors are, where you have to fight them head to head? Red water is shark infested. It is where the intense competition drives down margins to wafer-thin levels.

Blue-water strategy involves the exploration of new horizons rather than sticking with the existing ones. If you manage to find blue water you may not even need a competitive strategy, because there are no competitors.

Example
In 1978, Sony engineer, Nobutoshi Kihara, built a portable audio cassette for company chairman, Akio Morita, who wanted to be able to listen to operas during his frequent flying trips.

The product – the *Sony Walkman* – was then introduced in 1979, and it was so different from everything else available that, even in an intensely crowded market for portable music players, it had no competition whatsoever.

By the time competitors came in with similar products Sony had built up a massive lead. They had, in fact, found blue water. They have subsequently sold over 200 million units.

When you find blue water, it will probably pay not to be too greedy. Maintaining high margins will slow down your rate of growth and encourage competitors to enter.

Discovering blue water does depend on quite a high level of innovation. Once the market has been established, however, the blue-water company can enjoy high growth from a market leadership position.

Question mark

The fifth option is developing a strategic approach which is unique to you. It may involve a variation of, or combination of, the above. A hybrid strategy combining difference with lowest cost is very, very powerful.

Stuck in the middle

The biggest danger is not to have a clear strategy and to end up stuck in the middle. If you try to get a little bit of everything, or just not bother to think through a strategy, you will probably end up with no strategy at all.

GETTING COMMITMENT

The key to successful strategy implementation is getting the commitment of your team. More strategies fail because of a lack of commitment than anything else. They aren't necessarily wrong; it's just that people who matter simply haven't bought into them.

The more people there are involved in strategy development the better. Try to invite everyone in the business to contribute. Everyone, in some shape or form, should be asked what their views are and what they feel should be done. Most people will make no input but the fact they have been invited to increases the chance of them supporting the new strategy.

> ### TOP TIP
>
> Business strategy is principally creative. It requires 'blue-sky thinking'. Cast off the baggage of the past and try to look at everything in a new light.

Use the level-1 business plan builder.

Business strategy: level 3

This section follows on from levels 1 and 2. Everything in them must still be done at this level. Level 3 builds on the sophistication.

WIDENING YOUR SCOPE

At level 2 we looked at the choosing of a fundamental strategy. It may be that with a more complicated business there is a need for more than one strategy. This could be the case if vastly differing customer groups are being served, or vastly different product lines are in place.

This is rather dangerous, however, because it can end up with you being stuck in the middle or sending mixed messages to your marketplace. Look how focused Rolls Royce is. You just couldn't imagine them introducing a bargain-priced super mini! It's probably safer to choose one fundamental strategy and stick with it.

GROWTH

Most strategies are designed to help the business grow.

Igor Ansoff created his product market matrix in 1957. It remains a very useful tool that can be used when formulating a growth strategy (see Figure 11.4).

	Existing products	New products
Existing markets	Market penetration	Product development
New markets	Market development	Diversification

Figure 11.4   Ansoff matrix

Market penetration

The idea is to simply sell more of your *existing products or services to your existing customer groups*. Your revenue increases as a result of increased market share.

Growth can often come from understanding customers better than competitors do, and techniques explained at previous levels are helpful.

Other options are to increase expenditure on advertising and promotion, introduction of loyalty schemes, etc.

As the business continues to focus on products and markets that it knows very well, this is the *lowest-risk option*.

Market development

Find *new groups of customers* for your existing products.

A common example of this is venturing forth into new geographical areas. If that involves selling in another country, the business is entering a whole new ball game. There will probably be a whole new set of rules and regulations to comply with and, in addition, the customer may well be speaking a different language.

There may, of course, be an additional customer group on your own doorstep. You could, for example, be selling your DIY product to householders, while there may also be a demand in the trade for it.

As you know the product but not the market the *risk is probably medium to high*.

Product development

This strategy involves developing *new products for your existing customer groups*. How easy this is depends on how similar the new products are to your existing ones and whether you have sufficient competency in the organisation to produce them.

Once the product is developed, marketing it is relatively easy as you will be able to use your existing channels.

You are going to be producing products you are unfamiliar with but you know the markets and have your channels set up so the strategy carries *medium risk*.

Diversification

Here you are taking the bull by the horns and selling products you are unfamiliar with into markets you are unfamiliar with. Because of this, the strategy is *very high risk*.

Normally it doesn't make an awful lot of sense because the risks tend to outweigh the rewards.

If you really do want to diversify, it will reduce the risk if you are able to do it in two stages.

Reducing risk

Either:

1. Develop the new products you want for your new market but first introduce them to your existing market. *Medium risk*.
2. Develop the new market and introduce the now established new product. *Medium risk*.

Or:

1. Introduce some of your existing products into the market you want to diversify into. *Medium risk*.
2. Develop the new product and introduce into the now established new market. *Medium risk*.

	Existing products	New products
Existing markets	Market penetration	Product development
New markets	Market development	Diversification

Figure 11.5   Reducing risk

You are, in effect, replacing one high-risk move with two medium-risk moves by only tackling one unknown at a time.

Real life isn't always that simple, but the matrix does provide a good, commonsense guide when developing growth strategies.

Use the level-1 business plan builder.

12

Creating objectives

MONEY, MONEY, MONEY; IT'S THE RICH MAN'S WORLD

An objective is a goal the business is aiming for. Objectives are the principal difference between an external business plan and an internal business plan. An external reader is very interested in what has been achieved to date and what the general objectives for the future are, but the internal plan needs to cover them in a lot more detail. It is your blueprint for achieving your aims.

An external plan is generally produced to facilitate the raising of finance. The reader is the potential lender or investor in the business. The aim is to help you raise money which you eventually have to give back in one way or another. Other than financial targets, detailed objectives would not normally have to be included in an external plan. You can never really be sure an external plan won't get into the hands of a competitor and you hardly want to give them the recipe for your success!

An internal plan is for consumption within the organisation and is produced fundamentally to increase the amount of profit the business makes.

In other words, an external plan attracts money which you have to give back, while an internal plan attracts money you keep! When you think about it, creating an external plan without an internal companion makes little sense. An external plan compiled alongside an internal one is also easier to justify when funders start asking questions, as everything has already been thought through.

Figure 12.1   Hierarchy of objectives

ESTABLISHING YOUR HIERARCHY OF OBJECTIVES

The key planning mechanism for generating cash is the hierarchy of objectives (see Figure 12.1).

- **General aims** are long-term aspirations (10 years or more) that were covered in Chapter 10.

- **Business objectives** are the big headline objectives such as turnover and net profit. Start with three-year business objectives and cascade those down to one-year goals.

- **Business strategy** is the way the business objectives will be achieved.

- **Strategic objectives** are the targets the business strategy aims to achieve.

- **Functional objectives** are what each department (or function) has to achieve as its contribution to the realisation of the business objectives. They will be part of a functional (marketing, operations, etc.) plan.

- **Tactics** are the detailed short-term plans that the departments will use to achieve their functional objectives.

- **Team objectives** are what each team in the department has to achieve to realise the departmental objectives.

- **Milestone reviews** take place at predetermined intervals and are the interim monitoring devices of the plan. They often take place at monthly or three-monthly intervals. The milestone objective is what should be achieved by the next milestone date.
- **Goals, objectives and targets** are basically words that mean the same thing.

The key principle is that the objectives cascade down. Each one is a more detailed refinement of the higher level one above. Ultimately the higher-level objectives are achieved through the achievement of the ones below them.

MAKING IT SMART

The best objectives are SMART ones:

- Specific
- Measurable
- Achievable
- Realistic
- Time bound.

If they aren't SMART, you'll never really know whether you have achieved them or not because they are too fuzzy. What would you actually mean by: 'We want to improve customer satisfaction'? How would you tell when it was achieved?

Example

Our profit for year ending 31.3.2013 will be £3.2 million. This represents a 20% increase on the previous year.

Let's run a check.

- **S**pecific ✓ £3.2 million is very specific.
- **M**easurable ✓ To be measurable it needs to be expressed numerically, or else you'll never really know whether it has been achieved.

- **A**chievable ✓ A 20% increase on the previous year's performance looks very achievable. To have chosen a figure that everybody knew to be impossible would have been very demotivating.

- **R**ealistic ✓ A 20% increase represents a challenge for the team that has to be worked towards. Getting there will be a real achievement for all concerned and a cause for celebration. A 1% increase would also have been achievable, but it probably wouldn't have been a realistic challenge. Setting an objective so low that you are almost certain it will be achieved is not good for morale. It is pointless.

- **T**ime bound ✓ We have stated it to be for the year ending 31.3.2013. At that date we will know whether we have won or lost.

Objectives: level 1

SETTING YOUR BUSINESS OBJECTIVES

In your vision and mission you identified the long-term aims of the business. You were probably looking at a horizon of ten years or more in the future. It was a distant dream with no real detail.

When forming your vision and mission statement you were able to be idealistic. Now it is time to be specific and practical, to plan how to turn your ideals into what all businesses need to do: make money.

First, choose your medium-term horizon. The most common choice would probably be three to five years, but it could be as little as two if preferred. Our main concern here, however, will be the short term horizon which is usually 12 months.

The ultimate business objective is normally to make a profit. That is clearly going to be your primary focus, but growth in sales is, for most businesses, a key factor and that should be looked at as well.

Sales

Start by comparing last year's sales with the general aim in the vision/mission. What would sales need to be next year to represent good progress towards the vision?

Net profit

To calculate your net profit:

■ Start with last year's net profit (this is the bottom line – what is left after all the outgoings).

■ Calculate *percentage net profit*:

$$\% \text{ Net profit} = \frac{\text{Net profit}}{\text{Sales}} \times 100$$

■ Calculate *net profit* for next year assuming % net profit remains the same as last year:

$$\text{Net profit} = \text{Sales forecast} \times \% \text{ net profit}$$

or:

■ If you are planning to increase efficiency you can choose to target a higher net profit percentage.

■ Work out what the profit would be at the higher percentage:

$$\text{Net profit} = \text{Sales forecast} \times \text{Target } \% \text{ net profit}$$

Establish medium-term business objectives and then cascade them to one year business objectives.

BUSINESS STRATEGY

Development of your strategy for achieving your business objectives was covered in the previous chapter.

STRATEGIC OBJECTIVES

This is *what the business needs to achieve* in the period. The efforts of all the functions, departments and individuals should all contribute towards these.

Example

If business strategy is to increase sales by boosting customer loyalty, a strategic objective could be to reduce customer attrition by 50%.

FUNCTIONAL OBJECTIVES

The chosen business strategy now has to be broken down into functional objectives. That is not as difficult as it sounds.

The five basic functions are:

■ marketing
■ operations
■ people
■ finance
■ IT

We are attempting to turn the strategy (the way we are going to make our profit) into goals for each of the functions.

Example

Let's imagine that you fit central heating systems and your strategy is to increase profits by also starting to fit bathrooms for your existing customer groups (product extension). Your strategic objective is to fit 100 bathrooms over the coming year at an average price of £5,000, so your turnover from bathrooms is expected to be £500,000:

Functions	Objectives
Marketing:	Sell £500,000 of bathrooms in the next 12 months.
People:	Recruit and train sufficient people to sell, install and service 100 bathrooms over the next 12 months.
Operations:	Source bathroom products and ensure we have enough capacity to fit 100 bathrooms over the next 12 months (vehicles, equipment, etc.).
IT:	Do we need to upgrade any systems to cope with the additional workload?
Finance:	Ensure we have enough funding available to finance the above activities.

The functions are totally interdependent. Each depends on all the others to achieve its objectives to one extent or another. They certainly all depend on finance!

How each function achieves its objectives is dealt with in the functional chapters.

MILESTONES

Twelve months is usually too long to wait before monitoring your objectives. Wherever practical, try breaking 12-month objectives down into milestones. If you have said, for example, that you plan to sell 100 houses in the next 12 months, ask yourself how many should be sold in 3 months.

Make sure you actually review the plan at the milestone time. Military planners say that no plan survives first contact with the enemy. The milestone is your opportunity to take stock of what has actually happened and revise your plans accordingly.

Great generals are able to improvise and the same applies to managers. You need to have a good plan to start with, lest improvisation becomes fire fighting.

The most popular milestone period is three months, but some people go for one month, others four or six months. Decide what's right for you and put review dates in your diary. (Figure 12.2 gives a level-1 objectives plan builder.)

Objectives

Medium-term business objectives (3 years) from _____ to _____
Sales Profit
Short-term business objectives (1 year) from _____ to _____
Sales Profit
Strategic objectives

Functional objectives
   Marketing
   People
   Operations
   IT
   Finance

Figure 12.2   Objectives plan builder, level 1

TOP TIP

Remember, objectives are targeted results. Strategies are the means of achieving those results, and tactics are the detailed programmes that outline the actions that will be needed.

Objectives: level 2

In level 1 we took the long-term aim, which is big, and fairly unspecific maybe, into something well defined that will happen within the next year. We are now going to refine our medium-term planning.

SETTING YOUR MEDIUM-TERM OBJECTIVES

These lie in between the long-term aim and the short-term objectives. The medium-term objectives will probably have a horizon of two or three years at this stage. They are developed *before* the short-term objectives.

Your medium-term objectives should be milestones on the road to achieving your long-term aim. So clearly, the objective should be set somewhere between where you are now and where you want to be, say, 10 years in the future.

Example

If you are building 10 houses a year now and in 10 years' time you visualise building 100 houses a year, how many houses in year 3 would be seen as reasonable progress on that journey?

The logical, arithmetical approach would be to increase by 9 houses a year. However, increasing from 10 to 19 in year 1 would be much more difficult than increasing from 90 to 100 in year 10. Putting the greatest strain on the early years, when your experience is least, would make the project much more likely to fail.

It is better to look at percentages as this spreads the challenge over the whole 10 years evenly.

Table 12.1 can be used to calculate the annual growth rate needed. It is based on a start point of 1, which can be units or money.

Our example starts with 10 units, so all the figures in the table (except the growth %) need to be multiplied by 10. It ends with 100 units (which would be 10 in the

Table 12.1   Growth calculator

Growth (%)	Start	Year									
		1	2	3	4	5	6	7	8	9	10
5	1	1.05	1.10	1.16	1.22	1.28	1.34	1.41	1.48	1.55	1.63
6	1	1.06	1.12	1.19	1.26	1.34	1.42	1.50	1.59	1.69	1.79
7	1	1.07	1.14	1.23	1.31	1.40	1.50	1.61	1.72	1.84	1.97
8	1	1.08	1.17	1.26	1.36	1.47	1.59	1.71	1.85	2.00	2.16
9	1	1.09	1.19	1.30	1.41	1.54	1.68	1.83	1.99	2.17	2.37
10	1	1.10	1.21	1.33	1.46	1.61	1.77	1.95	2.14	2.36	2.59
11	1	1.11	1.23	1.37	1.52	1.69	1.87	2.08	2.30	2.56	2.84
12	1	1.12	1.25	1.40	1.57	1.76	1.97	2.21	2.48	2.77	3.11
13	1	1.13	1.28	1.44	1.63	1.84	2.08	2.35	2.66	3.00	3.39
14	1	1.14	1.30	1.48	1.69	1.93	2.19	2.50	2.85	3.25	3.71
15	1	1.15	1.32	1.52	1.75	2.01	2.31	2.66	3.06	3.52	4.05
16	1	1.16	1.35	1.56	1.81	2.10	2.44	2.83	3.28	3.80	4.41
17	1	1.17	1.37	1.60	1.87	2.19	2.57	3.00	3.51	4.11	4.81
18	1	1.18	1.39	1.64	1.94	2.29	2.70	3.19	3.76	4.44	5.23
19	1	1.19	1.42	1.69	2.01	2.39	2.84	3.38	4.02	4.79	5.69
20	1	1.20	1.44	1.73	2.07	2.49	2.99	3.58	4.30	5.16	6.19
21	1	1.21	1.46	1.77	2.14	2.59	3.14	3.80	4.59	5.56	6.73
22	1	1.22	1.49	1.82	2.22	2.70	3.30	4.02	4.91	5.99	7.30
23	1	1.23	1.51	1.86	2.29	2.82	3.46	4.26	5.24	6.44	7.93
24	1	1.24	1.54	1.91	2.36	2.93	3.64	4.51	5.59	6.93	8.59
25	1	1.25	1.56	1.95	2.44	3.05	3.81	4.77	5.96	7.45	9.31
26	1	1.26	1.59	**2.00**	2.52	3.18	4.00	5.04	6.35	8.00	**10.09**
27	1	1.27	1.61	2.05	2.60	3.30	4.20	5.33	6.77	8.59	10.92
28	1	1.28	1.64	2.10	2.68	3.44	4.40	5.63	7.21	9.22	11.81
29	1	1.29	1.66	2.15	2.77	3.57	4.61	5.94	7.67	9.89	12.76
30	1	1.30	1.69	2.20	2.86	3.71	4.83	6.27	8.16	10.60	13.79
31	1	1.31	1.72	2.25	2.94	3.86	5.05	6.62	8.67	11.36	14.88
32	1	1.32	1.74	2.30	3.04	4.01	5.29	6.98	9.22	12.17	16.06
33	1	1.33	1.77	2.35	3.13	4.16	5.53	7.36	9.79	13.02	17.32
34	1	1.34	1.80	2.41	3.22	4.32	5.79	7.76	10.40	13.93	18.67
35	1	1.35	1.82	2.46	3.32	4.48	6.05	8.17	11.03	14.89	20.11

table before multiplying), so look for the nearest figure to 10 in the right-hand column.

The closest is 10.09. That gives an annual growth of 26% and sales target for year 3 of (2.00 × 10) which is 20 units.

Use the calculator to work out the figures for your business. It will work for anything you can put a number to. Volume of units, sales revenue, market share: they all work. Just multiply the figures by your actual start point.

For example, if you start at 40 units a year, the year-6 figure at 10% increase is:

$$1.77 \times 40 = 71 \text{ units}$$

Templates are available from www.phct.co.uk. Simply enter your start point and get it calculated automatically. That way you can easily see what growth rate you need.

If the growth rate you calculate sounds too onerous, you will need to downgrade your long-term aim or stretch it further into the future. (Figure 12.3 gives a level-2 objectives plan builder.)

TOP TIP

Remember to include a lot more detail on your year-1, short-term objectives than on the medium-term ones. As the timeframe shortens the objectives get more detailed.

Objectives

Long-term aim (from Chapter 10)
Medium term. Timeframe: 3 years   from _____ to _____

3-year business objectives:
  Sales
  Net profit
  Gross profit
  Return on investment
(Choose the indicators that are right for you)

3-year strategy (from Chapter 11) (The strategy describes roughly how we will achieve the 3-year objectives. This gives us the opportunity to set changes in place that couldn't be made in 1 year)
Short term. Timeframe: 1 year   from _____ to _____

1-year business objectives:
  Sales
  Net profit
  Gross profit
  Return on investment

1-year strategic objectives:

Functional objectives:
  Marketing
  People
  Operations
  IT
  Finance

Figure 12.3   Objectives plan builder, level 2

Objectives: level 3

The long-term aims and business strategy are ultimately decided by top management. Whether or not that strategy will be successful depends, however, more on the workforce than on top management.

The first rule is that objectives should never be imposed upon people. People really resent being told what they have to achieve, especially when that something involves doing a lot more than they have been doing in the past. There is often an underlying, covert threat tied up with the under-achievement of the personal targets, and there is an escalation of mistrust. This environment generally leads to a likelihood of reduced rather than increased performance.

When the vast majority fail to reach their targets, management becomes sterile, and future targets become regarded with derision.

Discussions are needed between managers and team members about the way in which the individual is going to contribute to what the business is going to achieve. It is usually done in a combination of team and one-to-one meetings. Everyone's objectives are agreed and written down.

Top down, bottom up

It can be seen from Figure 12.4 how the long-term aims filter down to personal objectives. The key feature is the feedback loops. When the detail is worked out at the lower level, some objectives are seen to be impractical. This is due to circumstances which the higher, less detailed level had not identified. The feedback then facilitates modification of the objective so that it can actually be achieved. A common reason for amendment is that there is not enough resource to do everything intended in the timeframe anticipated.

There is a feedback loop from personal objectives up. This is very, very important. Individuals throughout the organisation should be encouraged to suggest new approaches and strategies. Nurtured correctly, this is a very rich vein of ideas that can have a massive impact on company efficiency and profitability.

125

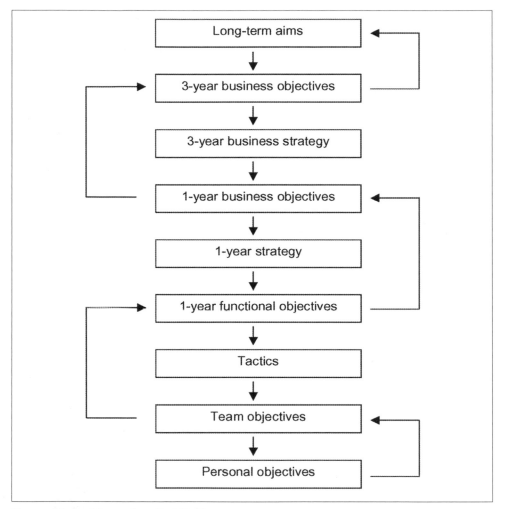

Figure 12.4   Hierarchy of objectives

This is a vibrant system that includes everyone in the organisation, values their opinions and is highly motivating. Everyone wants to be part of a winning team when they feel they have a voice. Many people may not choose to use it, but the fact they can makes all the difference.

Clearly not all ideas will be acted upon, but as long as people believe they have been considered and thanked for their contribution, they will continue to feedback in the future.

Business plan builder
Use the level 2 business plan builder.

13

Writing an effective marketing plan

It's easy to get marketing confused with business strategy.

Business strategy is concerned with identifying the groups of customers you are aiming at and building competitive advantage so those customers have more reason to buy from you than from competitors.

Marketing, on the other hand, involves contacting those potential customers and communicating the competitive advantage to them.

The marketing plan should tell the reader what mechanisms you are going to use to reach potential customers so that your objectives can be achieved.

Why you need it

Businesses need customers to survive. As reaching customers can be very expensive, a cost-effective marketing plan needs to be carefully thought through. Winning the right number of profitable customers is inevitably a make or break area of the plan, so potential investors will undoubtedly pay careful attention to this section.

Marketing plan: level 1

A lot of what has come before contributes to the marketing plan (see Figure 13.1).

After developing business objectives, headline marketing objectives were formulated (Chapter 12). Now is the time to explain how those marketing objectives are going to be achieved.

You will probably need to start by breaking down the headline objectives into sub-objectives or targets.

A popular way of doing this is to use the four 'P's: product, price, place and promotion. Emphasise any changes you intend to make.

Product (or service)

Explain exactly what you are selling. What are the unique selling propositions that will encourage customers to favour you over your opposition?

Try to think in terms of the whole package.

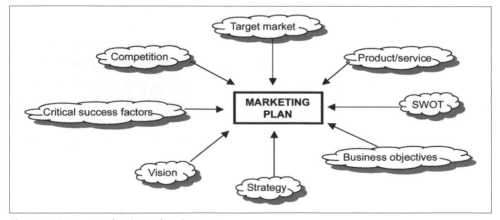

Figure 13.1   Marketing plan inputs

Example

You may be selling rubber ducks. The packaging may be better than that used by competitors so they turn up in better condition. You may have better display material for retailers so they are better presented. You may be supplying cleaning fluid with them which keeps them looking like new and leaves a film that helps them swim faster than those of your competitors. It's not just a rubber duck!

Price

What is your rationale for the pricing policy you have and where does that put you in the marketplace – i.e. are you a low, medium or high-price provider?

Place

What geographical area are you covering and where are your boundaries located? How are you going to distribute physically your product or service to customers?

Promotion

How exactly do you plan to communicate your message to prospective customers? This is very important as finding cost-effective promotional vehicles can be difficult. It's very easy to waste money on an advertising campaign, but selecting the right media with the right readership is critical for *cost-effective marketing*.

Example

One of your headline marketing objectives is to increase sales from £4 million to £5 million. This in itself is not very useful. In fact it can look quite frightening.

The first issue is where will that extra £1 million come from? Refer back to your strategy section and all should be revealed. Using that information, break down the objective. If your strategy is to get the extra turnover from new customers, you need to express how many new customers will be found.

Now determine where these extra customers will come from. Will you need to:

- Expand your product range?
- Change your pricing?

- Extend your geographic spread?
- Increase promotion?
- Employ more salespeople?

MARKETING BUDGET

Promotion, sales and distribution can cost a lot of money. Estimate what the cost will be month by month, so you know how much to allocate in your financial plan (see Figure 13.2).

Best practice is for the marketing director to justify all marketing expenditure from a zero base each year against the objectives aimed for. It's not good enough to say 'I need to spend this much more than last year because . . .'

Carry the bottom line forward to business plan builder.

Examples of cost items for the marketing department are as follows:

- **Personnel:** salaries, benefits, commissions and bonuses.
- **Market research.**
- **Communications:** advertising, branding, Internet marketing, website, PR, trade shows, etc.
- **Channels:** training distributors and paying commissions, etc.

Cost item	Jan	Feb	Mar	Apr	May	June	July	Aug	Sept	Oct	Nov	Dec	Total
Totals													

Figure 13.2   Marketing budget worksheet

- **Customer acquisition:** lead generation and customer loyalty.
- **Sundries and other costs.**

The worksheet won't appear in the marketing section of your plan, but the figures will go into your financial projections (see Chapter 16). The budget total figure can be mentioned in the marketing section.

CREATING YOUR SALES PLAN

Will you employ internal salespeople, external salespeople, will staff who are mainly employed to do something else sell when they have the time? An alternative may be to contract out the sales function. That way, however, you lose all-important contact with your customer base.

You can take the people element out of it by selling directly off your website or even by using good, old-fashioned mail order, but even then you may still need a telesales function to back it up.

A good start point is to look at what has worked for you in the past and take it from there. Break the sales forecast in the strategic plan down into sales for each product group and then break that annual figure down into monthly sales *taking account of seasonality*. (Figure 13.3 gives a sales plan worksheet.)

Carry the bottom line forward to the business plan builder. (Figure 13.4 gives a level-1 marketing plan builder.)

Product	Jan	Feb	Mar	Apr	May	June	July	Aug	Sept	Oct	Nov	Dec	Total
A B C													
Total													

Figure 13.3   Sales plan worksheet

Marketing Plan												
Product												
Price												
Place												
Promotion												
Selling												
Marketing budget												
Jan	Feb	Mar	Apr	May	June	July	Aug	Sept	Oct	Nov	Dec	Total
Sales plan												
Jan	Feb	Mar	Apr	May	June	July	Aug	Sept	Oct	Nov	Dec	Total

Figure 13.4   Marketing plan builder, level 1

TOP TIP

Use last year's marketing spend as your start point and add on any additional expenditure needed to fuel the growth you want; but you still have to justify the whole lot. After all, most of last year's spend could have been wasted!

Marketing plan: level 2

We will now revisit the four Ps but this time more strategically.

PRODUCT

Function
A successful product meets the needs of its customers better than its competitors do. How exactly does yours do this?

Finances
What is the overall financial impact of the product? Does it save the customer money in the long run? How does the overall cost of ownership compare with the competition?

Freedom
Will ownership gain your customers time or alleviate worry? How easy is it to buy and use?

Feelings
How does the product make customers feel about themselves? What is your brand image? How important is it that they like the salesperson?

Future
Will the products prove to be trouble free and if they do need servicing and support, will it be available?

PRICE

What is your pricing strategy and what is your cost base? If you want to be the lowest-priced supplier and you want to be successful, you also need to have the lowest-cost base in the market.

PROMOTION

Promotion isn't simply advertising. There are lots of ways to spend your promotional budget. Ensure you have the right mix so that you can reach your targets cost effectively.

Some examples:

- Advertising (press, specialist journals, TV, radio, etc.).
- Leaflets and flyers.
- Posters.
- Merchandising.
- Directories.
- Website.
- Search engines.
- Direct mail.
- Trade shows.
- Networking.

PLACE

Investigate the channels you can use.

Some examples:

- Your own retail outlets.
- Sales to retailers.
- Wholesalers.
- Direct marketing.
- Sales from website.
- Distributors.
- Agents.
- Strategic alliances.
- Field sales to end users.

Use the level-1 business plan builder form.

14

Developing your operations plan

Explain briefly how your business functions. If it's not obvious, you may need to say something about how your industry works. Stress any aspects of your operations that give you a competitive advantage. This may well stem from better methodologies or superior facilities that give you a cost advantage over your competitors.

Why you need it

You will need to convince the reader, and yourself, that you have the competency and capacity to deliver. Demonstrating how capacity will be adjusted to meet the needs of the plan boosts credibility.

Operations plan

The following are some of the issues that should normally be addressed. In each case it may be a good idea to draw comparisons with competitors.

Premises
Where is your head office, how many branches, how suitable and cost effective are the properties you currently use?

Processes
Outline the main production processes. These are systems you use to do the work from start to finish. What is special about yours?

Productivity
How efficient are you at producing your product or service? Do you have higher or lower costs than competitors? Why is this? What are you doing about it?

Quality
How do you maintain consistent quality of product? What systems do you have in place for dealing with customer complaints and how closely do you monitor them? How satisfied are your customers? How do you know this?

Stock
How much is tied up in raw materials, work in progress and finished goods? How does that compare with industry norms? How often do you suffer from not having the needed stock? Are you doing anything to improve the area of stock control?

Capacity
This is a critical area and cannot be glossed over. What volume of your various products and services do you currently have the capacity to produce?

Product	Last year's volume	Next year's volume	Current capacity	Increase/ (decrease) required
A				
B				
C				

Figure 14.1   Operational capacity worksheet

This is in terms of:

- equipment
- premises
- workforce.

How much spare capacity did you have last year? Do you have the capacity to produce what is forecast in the business plan? If you don't, what has to be changed to accommodate it and how much will it cost? (Figure 14.1 gives an operational capacity worksheet.)

How exactly will capacity be adapted? Explain the planned changes briefly and cost them.

ESTIMATING COST OF SALES

The forecasted sales have been calculated in the marketing plan. Now the cost of those sales can be estimated by looking at the operational implication (Figure 14.2).

Sales plan figures come from the marketing plan (Chapter 13).

OPERATIONS BUDGET

Figure 14.3 gives an operational budget worksheet.

Carry the bottom line forward to the business plan builder. Examples of cost items for the operations department are:

Sales plan													
Product	Jan	Feb	Mar	Apr	May	June	July	Aug	Sept	Oct	Nov	Dec	Total
A													
B													
C													
Cost of sales													
A Labour													
Materials													
Others													
B Labour													
Materials													
Others													
C Labour													
Materials													
Others													
Total													

Figure 14.2   Cost-of-sales worksheet

Cost item	Jan	Feb	Mar	Apr	May	June	July	Aug	Sept	Oct	Nov	Dec	Total
Totals													

Figure 14.3   Operational budget worksheet

- labour (recruitment, training, salaries and bonuses);
- premises;
- equipment; and
- others.

Example

Aldi is a company which has based its competitive advantage on operational efficiency. Supermarket customers are continually looking for high-quality products at the lowest prices possible.

The business has succeeded by aggressively reducing costs in all areas of the business. The business is run on the principles of lean operations. It comes directly from their mission:

Aldi's core purpose is to provide value and quality to our customers by being fair and efficient in all that we do.

Aldi's management is focused on getting more from less and passing those savings on to the customer. This is based on four fundamental programmes.

- **Continuous improvement:** constantly striving to get better
- **Just in time:** product received when needed to reduce stocking levels
- **Time-based management:** reduction of time wasted through a multi-skilled and flexible workforce.

Operations plan

Strategy

Changes required

Operations budget												
Jan	Feb	Mar	Apr	May	June	July	Aug	Sept	Oct	Nov	Dec	Total

Figure 14.4   Operations plan builder

■ **Total quality management:** everybody in the business is responsible for getting it right first time.

This philosophy has propelled Aldi into a very strong position with over 7,000 stores worldwide.

15

Describing management and skills

Your people plan is probably the most important part of the whole business plan. If the primary purpose of the plan is to raise money, focus on the strengths of the management team, as lenders and investors put more weight on this than anything else. They tend to be of the opinion that a very strong management team can make a weak strategy work but the strongest of strategies will probably come to nought if the team is weak.

If you want to grow and improve the business, skills throughout the organisation are crucially important. There have to be enough people with the required skills to make the plan come to fruition and crucially they need the inclination, the passion, and the drive to make it happen. To quote the immortal words of the famous sage, Bob the Builder, 'Can we do it?'

Focus on these key areas:

1. The management team.
2. The management structure.
3. Skills throughout the organisation.
4. Training budget.

If the plan is to raise money, especially if the business is a start-up, no. 1 is the most important but no. 2 should be covered briefly. If the aim is to improve the business (i.e. it's an internal plan) then your main focus should be on no. 3.

Management

DEFINING THE MANAGEMENT TEAM

These are the people who run your business. You need to demonstrate that your team has the required experience and skills to achieve the desired results. These skills don't have to all come from employees of the business. The team can be cost effectively strengthened by non-executive directors, consultants and advisers. If you have them, make sure you include them in this section of the plan.

You need to sell each member of your key management team by outlining their skills and experience (see Figure 15.1).

You can leave out the last point if you prefer. Including it does show objectivity and, as long as that quality is covered by another member of the team, it doesn't matter. You could also point out any planned development to overcome the weakness if necessary.

Planning for the future

You may decide to recruit new members to your management team. Outline the roles under vacancies, when you anticipate they will join and the salary you propose to offer. Add any additional salaries into your financial plan.

In a growing organisation the management team needs to change over time and roles will evolve. How do you anticipate this will happen and what are you going to do to prepare people for it?

```
Name
Position
Previous experience
Successes
Education
Strengths
Areas lacking strength
```

Figure 15.1   Management team worksheet

OUTLINING THE MANAGEMENT STRUCTURE

Describe how the business is or will be run. How will decisions be made, and by whom? Are there formal lines of authority with a hierarchy or is the organisation essentially flat with people at the coalface empowered to make decisions there and then? The easiest way to start is with an organisation chart.

TOP TIP

If you are using Microsoft Word: **Insert→Diagram→Organisation chart**.

Organisation chart

It can be seen from Figure 15.2 who reports to whom, backed up by your description of how the organisation ticks. You may decide to tuck the chart away in an appendix and just refer to it in the plan itself.

Management style

Each manager has a distinct management style. Some are hands on and controlling. They want to see everything going through themselves. Others are more trusting and focused on motivating and developing their team. They are happy to empower people and delegate.

The styles of individual managers should be compatible with the culture of the business as a whole. If the general culture is supportive, learning, no blame and empowering, a controlling, dictatorial manager would probably be a source of friction and the issue would probably need to be addressed eventually.

Describe briefly the management style and culture within the organisation.

SKILLS

If the business is well established, clearly there is a strong skills base already in place which has allowed it to perform at your current level. Most business plans seek to achieve improvement in performance and growth. The skills

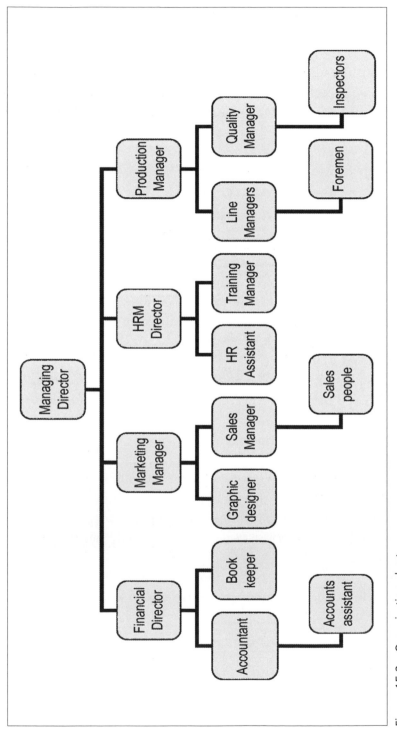

Figure 15.2 Organisation chart

the plan should focus on are those necessary to achieve that improvement and growth. If the business is a start-up, you have to look at everything.

It may be that you need more of what you have already got, or there could be a requirement for skills that are completely missing. This particularly applies to managers in a growing organisation, as the bar is being continually raised. Each year a learning organisation is better than it was before.

Look at the objectives for next year and ask yourselves what the additional demands will be from a people perspective. Can this skills gap be best bridged by:

- Training people you already have?
- Recruiting new employees?
- Making more use of consultants or advisers?
- Outsourcing part of your operation?

Go through your objectives with each of the functional managers/teams, establish the current shortfalls and explain briefly what you will do about them (usually choosing one of the four options above). (Figure 15.3 gives a skills worksheet.)

Training budget

Having determined your training needs, decide on timing and cost it on a month-by-month basis.

Function	Skill gaps	Action plan
Management Operations Technical Financial Marketing Personnel		

Figure 15.3 Skills worksheet

> ### TOP TIP
>
> Focus on the major skills gaps that you are planning to bridge. An investor would find a very long list of largely irrelevant skill shortages off-putting.

Figure 15.4 gives a management plan builder.

Management	
Management team	
Management structure	
Lines of authority	
Management style	
Skills requirements	
Vacancies	

Training budget												
Jan	Feb	Mar	Apr	May	June	July	Aug	Sept	Oct	Nov	Dec	Total

Figure 15.4   Management plan builder

16

Getting to grips with the finance

Most people feel apprehensive about tackling the numbers part of the plan. Without numbers, however, a plan would be meaningless. It would become a simple wish list that certainly would not impress a financier.

Getting to grips with the basic business numbers will not only improve your chances of raising the funding you need for your new project, but will also make your business easier to manage.

You can certainly enlist the help of your accountant for this part if you wish, but you will still need to understand the numbers before you can justify the plan to an investor or lender.

Why you need it

Viewers of the popular TV show *Dragon's Den* will be only too aware of the reaction suffered by people who do not understand the numbers. Business is primarily about making a profit. Financial control is vital to this.

Finance

The buzz words

- **Gross profit**: what you are left with after direct costs are paid.
- **Direct costs**: cost of materials, cost of labour directly incurred when producing the product or service and commissions.
- **Fixed (indirect) costs**: costs you can't attribute to a particular product or job. This includes: administrative, labour and overheads.
- **Net profit**: what's left after all expenditure (direct and indirect).
- **Capital expenditure**: items that should last more than a year (e.g. office equipment).

CREATING YOUR PROFIT AND LOSS FORECAST

When you are in business you generally buy and sell. You buy the raw materials you use and then sell them as the finished article. The problem is that the profit you make is not simply the difference between the price you pay for something and the price you sell it for. There are a whole load of other things you have to buy in the mean time. You may need equipment, premises, staff and have other costs. Some of those costs are directly related to the job (such as materials) but others have to be paid whether you have work or not (such as premises). This applies to all types of businesses.

Even though you may be selling for considerably more than you are buying, you will lose money if your profits are insufficient to cover your costs.

The profit and loss (P & L) forecast (Figure 16.1) enables you to estimate what your profit or loss will be for the level of sales you anticipate. If the answer is a loss, look at what can be changed to turn that into a profit. This is a lot less painful than trial and error. Investors certainly aren't prepared to allow you to take that approach with their money, and that's why they want to see a forecast.

Name of business

Projected Profit and Loss

	Jan	Feb	Mar	Apr	May	Jun	Jul	Aug	Sep	Oct	Nov	Dec	Total
SALES													
COST OF SALES													
Materials													
Direct labour													
Distribution													
Commissions													
TOTAL COST OF SALES													
GROSS PROFIT													
GROSS PROFIT %													
OVERHEADS													
Indirect wages and salaries													
Directors' remuneration													
Premises costs													
Office costs													
Travel													
Sundries													
Bank costs													
Depreciation													
TOTAL													
NET PROFIT/LOSS													
NET MARGIN %													
CUMULATIVE b/f													
CUMULATIVE c/f													

For direct labour, wages and salaries and directors' costs: include PAYE, NI and any benefits

Figure 16.1 Projected P & L

The primary difference between a P & L and a cash-flow forecast is one of timing. In the P & L it doesn't matter *when* money goes in or out, so it can be a simpler way to start.

The forecast for the first year is generally done monthly and for the second and third years, quarterly. If you are doing fourth and fifth years, they would be annual, but that far ahead forecasting can be fairly meaningless and you will find that for most applications three years is enough.

Your sales forecast will come from the marketing plan worksheet (Chapter 13). Get the cost of sales (variable costs) from the operations plan worksheet (Chapter 14). Add any non-production direct costs such as sales commissions.

Now insert figures for your fixed costs. These are business expenses that do not depend on the volume of products or services supplied. They are not permanently fixed as they will change over time, but in the very short term they have to be paid even if you sell nothing, so they can be something of a millstone:

- For direct labour, wages, salaries and directors' remuneration, include PAYE, NI and any benefits.
- Premises costs: include rent, rates, power, etc.
- Depreciation: capital purchases have a long life and, for P & L purposes, you should write them down over their lifetime in a meaningful way. Typical amounts are:
  - ☐ Computer equipment and software: 3 years ($\frac{1}{3}$ cost each year).
  - ☐ Office equipment: 5 years ($\frac{1}{5}$ cost each year).
  - ☐ Building works: 10 years ($\frac{1}{10}$ cost each year).

There are other ways to do it but this is the simplest. You may want to discuss this with your accountant. Please note: depreciation for taxation purposes is different and amounts are set by HMRC.

You can download the template for Excel from the PHCT website or create your own, www.phct.co.uk.

CASH-FLOW FORECAST

The cash-flow forecast is probably the most important financial document in the plan. A business can be highly profitable but, if it does not have sufficient cash to pay its bills, it will fail. The forecast identifies *in advance* when there are going to be cash shortages. It is easier to make provision for this in advance than it is to cope with an immediate crisis:

- **Sales:** start with P & L figures and adjust for any delay in receiving payment. Include any expected payments for sales made in prior year.
- **Issue of shares:** investment by shareholders. If you receive funding from outside investors in return for shares or if existing shareholders purchase additional shares, it goes here as does your initial investment.
- **Loans:** this is money borrowed which has to be repaid.
- **VAT refunds:** VAT refunds received from HMRC.
- **Capital expenditure:** use 100% of cost in the month you pay for it.
- **Materials.**
- **Distribution.**
- **Commission:** get figures from P & L and adjust to month in which payment will be made.
- **Overheads.**
- **Corporation tax and loan repayment:** if you are not sure yet what they will be, it's probably better to leave blank.

Figure 16.2 gives an example of a cash-flow template. An Excel template can be found at www.phct.co.uk.

BALANCE SHEET

This shows the value of a business at a particular point in time. Investors are particularly interested in what a business is worth and this is an indication. What the business would be worth if it were sold would probably be different, however. The written-down 'book value' of assets in the balance sheet may not equate to their market value and buyers are generally prepared to pay a goodwill premium.

Name of business
Projected cash flow

	Jan	Feb	Mar	Apr	May	Jun	Jul	Aug	Sep	Oct	Nov	Dec	Total
INCOME													
SALES													
Issue of shares													
Loans													
VAT reclaim													
TOTAL INCOME													
OUTLAY													
Capital expenditure													
Materials													
Direct labour													
Distribution													
Commissions													
Overheads (less depreciation)													
Input VAT													
Corporation tax													
Loan repayments													
TOTAL OUTLAY													
NET CASH FLOW													
OPENING CASH b/f													
CUMULATIVE CASH c/f													

Figure 16.2 Projected cash flow

If yours is an existing business you should be able to get the current values from your last set of published accounts, and then project forward using your projected P & L, anticipated expenditure, etc. With a new business you start from nothing. You may have to include draft accounts for the most recent period if they have not yet been published.

Fixed assets:

- **Cost**: existing assets at cost plus anticipated capital expenditure.
- **Depreciation**: accumulated over time.
- **Stock**: estimated value at end of period.
- **Debtors**: monies still due for goods supplied at end of period.
- **Cash at bank**: expected value. Use cash-flow forecast.

Current liabilities:

- **Trade creditors**: money you owe at end of period.

Figure 16.3 gives an example of a projected balance sheet template. An Excel template can be found at www.phct.co.uk.

SENSITIVITY

What would be the impact of sales being, say, 10% lower or costs being 5% higher? Try reworking the 12-month P & L with various changes in place to help you evaluate the impact of changes.

BREAK EVEN

This is the level of sales at which *profit falls* to zero. Look at the sensitivity results and try various sales reduction levels to calculate your breakeven point. You can use your P & L or the PHCT sensitivity worksheet to do this very easily. Just try different values of (O4) until (N23) becomes zero.

If a 5% reduction in sales resulted in breakeven, the project would be considered very risky. If the reduction for breakeven was 50% the project would be very resilient.

Name of business
Projected Balance sheets

FIXED ASSETS
Cost
Less depreciation
Total fixed assets
CURRENT ASSETS
Stock
Debtors
Cash at bank
Total current assets
Total Assets
CURRENT LIABILITIES
Trade creditors
Tax payable
Short term loans
Total current liabilities
LONG TERM LIABILITIES
Loans
Total liabilities
Net Assets

REPRESENTED BY
Shareholders capital
Profit and Loss a/c

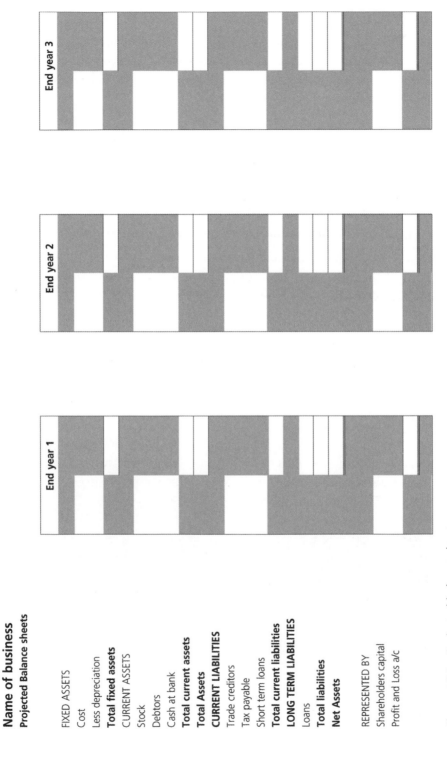

Figure 16.3   Projected balance sheet

ASSUMPTIONS

When you create a forecast you are essentially taking a view of an uncertain future. No one knows what exactly is going to happen next week, next month or next year.

The only way you can create a forecast is by *assuming* that the future will unfold in a particular way. You may take a view that:

- the general economy of the country will stay roughly the same, improve or decline;
- there will be no change in the level of competition you face;
- your costs will increase or decrease by a certain percentage; or
- the market for your product or service will stay the same, fall by a percentage or rise by a percentage.

To give credibility to your plan you must state your assumptions and cite any research you have carried out as a basis for your decision. You are, in essence, basing your plan on an expectation of what an uncertain future will bring. No one really knows whether your assumptions will be right or wrong but you must say exactly what they are.

They can be based on research you have carried out, your experience of the business, or more probably a combination of the two. (Figure 16.4 gives an assumptions worksheet.)

Assumptions	Basis

Figure 16.4   Assumptions worksheet

TOP TIP

It's much easier to use a spreadsheet.

Figure 16.5 gives a finance plan builder.

1. Prepare P & L forecast
2. Prepare cash-flow forecast
3. Prepare projected balance sheets
4. Sensitivity analysis
5. Breakeven analysis
6. Assumptions

Figure 16.5   Finance plan builder

17

Getting results

This is the most important part. Even if your primary reason for creating a business plan is to raise finance for a new project, it is still vitally important that the project subsequently succeeds.

Assuming you have written a great plan and obtained the financial support you needed, there are two vital elements that will help you achieve the results you crave: regular reviews and involving your team. If you neglect these, the chances are that your lovingly crafted plan will forlornly sit on a shelf and achieve nothing.

CARRYING OUT REGULAR REVIEWS

Planning a business is similar to planning a military campaign. Helmuth van Moltke (1800–1891) was a German Field Marshall and was widely regarded as one of the greatest strategists of warfare. He believed that military strategy was simply a system of options, since only the beginning of an operation was plannable. Famously he said that no plan survives first contact with the enemy.

If we don't expect the plan to survive first contact with the enemy, what is the point of planning? In the research I carried out for this book, when I asked people running small businesses for their view on planning, this issue came up over and over again. What is the point of planning when it never works out as you have planned?

The answer is that if you don't plan, you put yourself at a massive disadvantage compared with competitors who do. Even if they have got their forecasts and assumptions for the future wrong, they will still have considered carefully how to leverage their assets to maximum effect. Then when they see the result of first contact they will *adapt their strategy accordingly*. Strategy is always developed with imperfect information, but as the plan unfolds that information becomes perfect. The sensible manager takes advantage of that.

If we return to the military scenario, and one leader has 10,000 men while the other has 9,000, with armaments being similar; without strategy the force of 10,000 will always win. However, a force of 10,000 men with a very weak strategy can very easily be beaten by a force of 5,000 men with a strong strategy.

It is the same with business. Having greater resources counts for little if the strategy pursued is vastly inferior to that of a competitor. When Virgin Airways took on the giants, there should only have been one winner. Virgin, however, had a stronger strategy and has subsequently won more and more market share.

MILESTONES

Completing your business plan should result in a detailed 12-month plan with objectives, strategy and intended tactics spelt out.

For it to work, the plan now needs to be used in the day-to-day running of the business. It should be a blueprint of how to run your business that can be referred to on a regular basis.

That in itself is not enough. You must also set aside times when you will carry out a formal review of the plan. A well established business should do this at least quarterly, while a new business should do it at least monthly.

Go through your 12-month objectives and determine what needs to be achieved by your first milestone date, for you to achieve your 12-month objective on time. Only do this for the first milestone. The second milestone is created on the first milestone date.

Example

You have decided that a quarterly review is appropriate. First, set up the 3-month milestone objectives only. At that milestone, review performance to date, decide on changes, and then formulate your 6-month milestone objectives. Some individuals will clearly have made more progress with their objectives than others. This is your opportunity to determine who needs assistance before deadlines are missed.

What you will have is a rolling programme as shown in Figure 17.1.

When you review the results, you need to determine the reasons for under or over-achievement. Unexpected deviations will often be caused by outside influences that were not anticipated. Once you have determined the cause you know more than you knew when you wrote the plan originally and it is now out of date. Do not be afraid to change your plan in light of this new information. The most important thing to remember is that plans are not written in stone. They should be dynamic documents that reflect your current view of the world. (Figure 17.2 gives a milestone worksheet.)

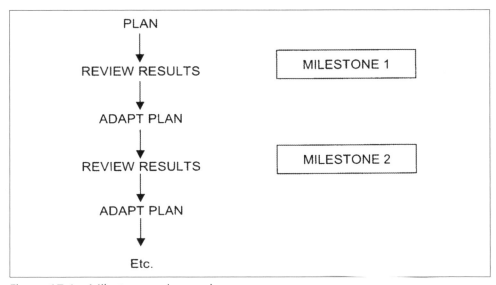

Figure 17.1   Milestone review cycle

Milestone date:	
12-month objective	Milestone objective

Figure 17.2   Milestone worksheet

END-OF-YEAR REVIEW

The main review takes place annually, when the three-year plan gets expanded another year and the next 12 months is planned in detail, using what has been learnt in the enactment of last year's plan.

INVOLVING THE TEAM

Planning does not work when it is done in isolation. When the top team gathers in a secret huddle to formulate the plan and then keep it to themselves, it is virtually guaranteed not to work. Yet so many organisations make this mistake.

The more people there are involved in the planning process the better. After all, everyone working in the business should be contributing in some way or other to the achievement of the plan. If they are not, why are they still working there, and what are they actually doing?

Communication

One of the big benefits of a great planning system is that it boosts communication. One of the greatest causes of discontent in a workforce is a lack of knowledge of what is going on. Proponents of 'mushroom management' rarely have a motivated workforce. The mantra of mushroom management is: 'Keep them in the dark and feed them dung.'

Everyone working in your business is affected by your plan, so everyone should understand it; know what their role is and how their part fits into the whole. This is the strongest way of making your plan work and creating a motivated workforce, all pulling in the same direction – towards achieving the business objectives.

Members of the top team will undoubtedly be the ones who formulate the plan, but it is the people at the coalface who will ultimately make it happen or not. Eliciting their opinion on parts of the plan which affect them is vital because they often have specialist knowledge and experience lacking in the top team. If there is a reason why something you plan cannot work, the sooner you know about it the better.

When you have formulated your first stab at a strategy, it is helpful to organise a series of short meetings so you can tell everyone what you are planning to do, while encouraging comments and ideas.

At the lower levels of the workforce you may not get a lot of input, but people really do appreciate being a part of the process and not being kept in the dark. When they feel that the formulation has involved them and they have been asked their opinion, people are more likely to take ownership of the plan and strive to make it work. It is also sometimes surprising where good ideas come from.

Hierarchy of objectives

The basic process was explained in Chapter 12. It is essential that each individual in the organisation knows exactly what their contribution to the achievement of business objectives will be. The business objectives need to be broken down into functional objectives, then team objectives and finally personal objectives.

For team objectives to happen the team leader must first understand what the team needs to achieve over the next 12 months as its contribution to the business objectives. Then the leader would probably discuss what needs to be achieved with the team and between them decide how exactly it will be done, and what additional resources will be needed, if any.

There will often be a combination of team meetings and one-to-one meetings. As a simple example: if an objective is to increase sales of product A by 20% and the team is in dispatch, they will need to discuss how they plan to get 20% more of that product through the system. Will the current workforce be able to handle it, will they need more space, etc.?

Each individual should agree what their contribution will be and, if appropriate, SMART objectives should be set (Chapter 12).

Appraisal system

If you operate a staff appraisal system it should become part of the business planning process.

The appraisal interview is a good vehicle for agreeing an individual's contribution to the plan. It's an opportunity to discuss the goals the individual will set and what their needs are in terms of training or other support to ensure that those objectives are met.

Business planning should really be a development exercise for all concerned. Year by year the capability of the organisation should increase, so more can be achieved this year than last year.

Bottom-up feedback

The team leaders should estimate their resource needs for the plan to be achieved, including any training for individuals that is necessary for the skills boost that may be needed to achieve the extra demands.

Once the top team have satisfied themselves that the resource demands are reasonable, they have to find the budget to fund them or modify the objectives to a level that can be afforded. There is no point in trying to achieve something for which the necessary resource is not available.

Unfortunately, company politics often raises its ugly head here, and some individuals may see this as an opportunity for self-aggrandisement. Everyone should be working as a team for the benefit of the organisation as a whole. Self-serving attitudes should not be allowed to prevail. If it becomes clear that an individual is trying to sabotage the plan, disciplinary action should immediately follow. You would probably be better off without an individual who is not prepared to work for the benefit of the organisation.

The performance of each and every individual should ideally be reviewed at each milestone. Underperformance is often down to people and you should have an idea of who is falling behind, and why, when you attend a top-level milestone meeting.

Clearly this process needs to fit into the prevailing culture of the business and the personalities of individuals involved. It does, however, provide a good recipe for managing the performance of an organisation. (Figure 17.3 shows the top-down, bottom-up loop.)

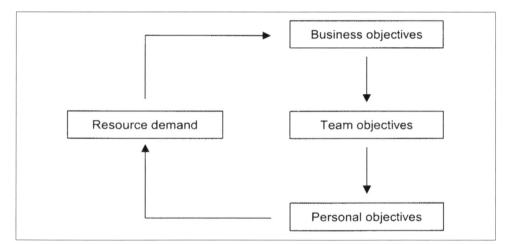

Figure 17.3   Top-down, bottom-up loop

18

Gaining acceptance

YOUR READER

Most business plans are written with at least one reader in mind. The plan is generally intended to persuade that reader to do something. Your reader could be:

■ a bank manager from whom you want approval for a new line of credit;

■ a potential investor you want to convince; or

■ your workforce, and you want them to support your planned initiatives.

MAKING A PITCH

In addition to providing them with a plan many readers will also want you to make a pitch. This means saying why someone should commit to it and asking for what you want.

The pitch can take place in different ways:

■ email

■ letter

■ telephone

■ face to face.

The method of communication may vary, but the message is essentially the same. You have to be succinct and persuasive. Tell them what's in it for them, what exactly you want (it may not just be money) and tell them when they will get their money back. You will probably need to convince them that they actually will get their money back!

THE MEETING

Make sure you arrive prepared. Have your facts and figures to hand and ensure that you have a full understanding of them. You will be asked questions and waffled answers would be the kiss of death.

You will probably be asked to give them a run-through of the plan. Again, waffling away for half an hour will probably not be helpful. You need to prepare your talk in advance and practise it.

A PowerPoint presentation can be effective. It's a great way to plan your talk, and the slides keep you on track. Tell them in advance you are going to use PowerPoint and make technical arrangements. If you are presenting to just one person taking along a laptop computer and simply using its screen should suffice.

The presentation will be a distillation of your plan, but it must also focus on your proposal.

THE PROPOSAL

The business plan itself can be thought of as a supporting document for the proposal. The proposal sets out exactly what you are asking the reader to do and the business plan backs it up.

If you want different things from different people, create a unique proposal for each of them. Best results can be obtained by tweaking your standard business plan for each reader. Emphasise aspects they will be particularly interested in, and omit or cut back sections with little relevance (more advice in Chapter 1).

The proposal shouldn't be a long document, a maximum of a couple of pages or so should suffice. *There is no need to repeat the detail from the plan; just summarise.*

The proposal could be the basis of a letter that accompanies the plan.

ELEMENTS OF THE PROPOSAL

What you are planning to do

This needs to be summed up in a nutshell. It should only be a few sentences. This is not as easy as it sounds, and it may involve the need to clarify your own thoughts as to what the key issues are.

How will it be done?

The detail is obviously in the plan. Here you have to sum it up concisely. By getting an understanding of what the key activities are, you will increase the likelihood of the readers saying 'yes' and improve your chances of succeeding with the project.

Where it will be done

Location is important. In retail it is everything and for all other businesses it is the key determiner of logistics, market coverage and can also be a major cost item. Finding and equipping the right premises can also take a long time, so it can have a significant effect on the project's timescale.

Timescale

When you need the money, when production will start and when investors can expect to get their money back, are very important considerations. If you do not have clear expectations of what these dates will be, the reader will be less inclined to support you.

Why you will succeed

The key thought going through the reader's mind is probably, 'is this going to work?' At this stage you need to be pretty confident that it is going to work. Explain exactly why you believe it will work. This is a great exercise in itself. Thinking it through very carefully may highlight some weakness in the plan. If it does, go back to the plan and try to eliminate those weaknesses. *This single little trick can save you thousands of pounds and many sleepless nights!*

ASKING FOR WHAT YOU WANT

You need to be absolutely sure about what you need and how exactly you are going to use it. A lender certainly isn't going to be happy to fund your next holiday!

There are different ways of raising money. You may find that you need a mix of different mechanisms. The two main categories are as follows:

- **Loan:** the lender gives you a specific amount of money, usually for a pre-agreed length of time and will expect repayments of the amount borrowed and interest. In the case of a fixed-term loan, the repayments will take place at regular intervals over the life of the loan. It is a good way of funding the purchase of capital equipment. An overdraft is open ended and normally used for working capital. The main concern of the lender is whether you will be able to pay the money back as agreed. Because of this lack of certainty, the lender will often ask for security.
- **Equity:** the investor is buying a part of your business and will eventually expect to be able to sell the shares received at a profit. The investor is looking to see your business grow and generate profits, so is viewing the business from a totally different perspective than a lender is. For this method, your business has to be a limited company.

At this stage there is no need to try to work out the package you want. Simply ask the investors for the amount required and see what is offered by each. Investors can bring more than money to the table; they may have a lot of invaluable experience and expertise.

You do need to think about the value you are going to place on the business. If, for example, you are looking to raise £100,000 and for that you are offering 10% of the business, you are valuing your business at £1 million. You will clearly need to justify that valuation of £1 million, when the investor asks how it was worked out.

If £100,000 is needed through equity, and the business is actually worth £500,000, it will probably be necessary to offer 20%.

167

Unrealistic valuations are a massive turn-off for professional investors, so make sure you have your figures right. This is something you may want to discuss with your accountant if you are going for a sizeable equity package.

If you specifically want the investor to help with the running of the business or offer advice on an ongoing basis, be sure to include it in the proposal.

The proposal can be aimed at people whose co-operation you are looking for without financial involvement, such as suppliers, members of staff, owners of premises, etc.

Your investment

Explain exactly what you and any other existing investors have invested to date and what exactly the current ownership of the business is. This is very important. The funder needs to know exactly who owns what percentage of the business.

You will also need to state what new investments have already been secured towards the package you are looking for, and the effect that will have on the ownership of the business.

Your investment doesn't necessarily have to be in the form of money. You may already have worked for 12 months in the business for a very low salary. You may want to commit to working for another 12 months at a very low salary. You may be bringing a patented product into the business. All these can be costed and included as part of your investment, but don't be too greedy, as over-evaluating your contribution is a big turn-off for investors.

Summarise the planned package showing exactly what you are looking for.

Example

New funding for expansion programme:

From existing directors	100,000
Other existing investors	75,000
Suppliers	50,000
Loans	100,000
Subtotal	325,000

Funds required	175,000
Total requirement	500,000

The proposal will clearly be for the raising of the £175,000 still required.

EXPLAINING THE EXIT PLAN

Explain the return the investor is likely to get and when they will get it. Professional investors tend to look at a timescale of three to five years before getting their money back. They may receive dividends from their shares, interest on any loans and directors' fees along the way, but the major part of their return will probably come from selling their shares some time in the future.

You will need to show them how they will be able to sell those shares. Common ways of doing this are through:

- a trade sale;
- a sale to a second-stage investor;
- a sale to a new working partner; or
- a stock market flotation.

A trade sale is probably the most common exit mechanism. Stock market floatation would only be a feasible option for a sizeable business. Indicate the exit timeframe you have in mind.

THE ELEVATOR PITCH

Many professional investors ask for an elevator pitch. The idea is that you convey the main gist of the proposal in the time you would spend in an elevator with someone – maybe 30 seconds! This really is a challenge in brevity and persuasion.

> ### TOP TIP
>
> Remember the fact that the proposal needs to be persuasive and convey what the interested party stands to gain from it.

169

19
Start-up business plans

A start-up plan is arguably the most difficult to create. A start-up is a new business with no track record.

In the case of an ongoing business you have past performance to extrapolate from. While taking last year's result and adding an arbitrary percentage for growth is definitely not recommended under any circumstances, last year's performance does give a benchmark of what next year's results would be if nothing in the business was changed and trading conditions remained static. The anticipated effect of intended changes on the benchmark could then be estimated quite accurately. Using that methodology existing businesses can produce very accurate forecasts, even in a rapidly growing organisation.

Start-ups begin with a blank sheet of paper. Often there is not as great a knowledge of the market as there would be in an established business. Resultantly the forecasts produced by many start-ups are hopelessly inaccurate.

The following comments will show you how to adapt the instructions, chapter by chapter, to create a start-up business plan and should be read in conjunction with the relevant chapters.

CHAPTER 3: SAMPLE PLAN

The sample plan has been done for an established business. The same format can be used for a start-up but there are some obvious differences. There are the adaptations that need to be made for a start-up. Of course next year and thereafter yours will be an established business and you can revert to the approach of the sample.

Business description

In *business details* insert where you are planning to start trading from. If you plan to start from home that's fine: just put your home address in. If you haven't got a web domain name, consider getting one.

Don't be afraid to be too ambitious in your *mission statement*; you do have a blank canvas to work with which can be an advantage.

Ownership, management and legal status and funding. Enter the names of all the proposed owners, the initial investment each will make, what that investment will comprise (one partner could be putting a van worth £3,000 into the business, for instance). State the proposed legal structure of the business (there is no need to incorporate before getting your funding), and what percentage each owner will receive. Please note that if you are planning to give equity to outside investors the business will need to be incorporated so you can issue shares. If you are not sure about this, talk to your accountant.

Achievements to date. Because you've not started doesn't mean you have no achievements. Have you thought of a better way of doing something, designed a new product, produced your first prototype, won a patent, arranged exclusive distributorship of a great product, or convinced a major retailer to stock your product? There is a lot to do before starting and the further down that path you are the more an investor is likely to be impressed.

Products and services

You probably don't actually have any products or services yet but you certainly should have some planned! You need to explain the range you plan to start with and what point product development is at for each product or service. Stress any relevant prior experience in your team.

Past experience really is very important in a start-up. If you have done exactly what you are proposing to do for another organisation, you will undoubtedly have a head start.

Market structure

Demonstrating an understanding of the market is vital in a new enterprise. Be absolutely clear as to who your customer will be. Not focusing enough is very dangerous for a start-up as you have limited resources to work with and run the risk of making very little impact.

Look at your past experience along with the resources available and try to work out what type of customer you are in the best position to satisfy.

Competition

Underestimating the competition is a common start-up mistake. Even if members of staff have worked for large players in the industry, those enterprises may not be the main competitors.

Research before you start. Know who your direct competitors will be and what their strengths and weaknesses are.

Also think about how they may react to your entering the market. Start-ups often underestimate the response of established players to their entering the market.

Strategy

You have a clean sheet of paper, so be creative. How are you going to win in this marketplace? An investor or a funder will be looking for a strong strategy. Try to think of something better than undercutting competitors.

How are customers' needs not being catered for in the marketplace? What are you going to do better than the existing players?

What are the risks when you enter this marketplace and what are you going to do to counter them?

Business objectives

This is very difficult for a new business as you have no previous trading to go by. Think about what *capacity* you are going to start with and how you will sell that volume of work. When calculating capacity, remember to allow time for sales and administration. There is more to running a business than doing the work!

Use the profit and loss forecast to work out what levels of profit you can expect at various levels of turnover, bearing in mind the costs you anticipate.

You are probably not going to get it right first time. Reviewing progress after a month or so is vital. Then you can make adaptations to your plans that have come from real experience.

Within 12 months of starting, most new businesses have changed their business model. Understand this, be flexible and be prepared to rewrite your business plan after a couple of months if necessary.

Marketing plan

This is where you distil your strategy down into what you are actually going to do to promote your business and how much it's going to cost. As you probably don't have a big budget you will need to think very carefully about what you will do.

Lots of new businesses do it cheaply, using methods such a getting friends and family to deliver leaflets. Make sure it's focused on your target and that it's cost effective. Be prepared to adapt your approach in light of experience.

Management and skills

This is really important. Many investors cite this as the most important thing they look at. Nobody in the business when it starts has any experience of working in this business. Everyone has experience picked up elsewhere. It is essential that the reader understands what the transferrable skills are.

Transferrable skills are picked up in one environment and then prove to be useful in a different environment. Think about the skills and experience present in the team you plan to start with and work out which essential skills are not covered.

You cannot afford to employ people with all the necessary skills from the start but you can attend training courses and use professional advisers.

Your accountant should have a wealth of experience and can be used for more than just preparing your annual accounts. Specific projects such as setting-up processes and systems can be carried out by consultants with the necessary skills.

Free management training and advice is generally offered by government agencies to start-up businesses.

Operations

You may already know how to produce your product or service. Think it through; you may only have been exposed to part of the process in your previous employment. It's the bit you weren't aware of that's likely to trip you up.

Financials

For many this is the hardest part. Use the templates and translate what you've developed in your plan into numbers.

If you need help, speak to your accountant or local enterprise agency.

CHAPTER 4: MARKET STRUCTURE

Investors know that people who start businesses with a good understanding of the market they will be operating in are more likely to succeed. Achieving that understanding *and demonstrating you have it*, will most definitely increase the likelihood of winning that all-important funding.

For most start-ups level 1 should suffice. Most of the content applies equally to both start-ups and existing organisations.

Narrowing your target market is important, as a start-up generally has limited resources and focusing on too wide an area will dilute the impact of your marketing efforts. Remember that your plan is not cast in stone and that you can change your target in the light of experience if the worst comes to pass, but it is still important to have a clear focus when you start.

You will have no customer records from which to fill in the customer analysis worksheet. You can, however, do it for your main competitors. From what you know about them, estimate what their target markets are and try to find gaps for yourself.

As a new business you probably do not want to compete head to head with your established competitors from the start if you can avoid it. Try to find groups of customers who are not being properly catered for in the existing market. That way, it is easier to gain a foothold.

CHAPTER 5: THE COMPETITION

Everything in this chapter applies to start-ups. As a start-up business you are almost certainly at the disadvantage of knowing less about your competitors than they know about each other. So at this stage you have more work to do.

It's like a detective mystery. Think about how you can find the information you need. You may have worked in the industry as an employee. You will certainly know a lot about the companies you have worked for. You will probably be recruiting staff who have experience in the industry. You will be talking to prospective suppliers who are supplying your competitors. You are probably already talking to prospective customers who are being supplied by your competitors. Your professional advisers probably have knowledge of the market. Talk to someone from your local enterprise agency.

As a start-up you are starting with a clean sheet of paper. It would be foolish to compete head on with strong, established competitors if you can avoid it. Knowledge of your competitors can tell you what their weaknesses are, what part of the market they are not catering for properly. By focusing on the customers your competitors are not really interested in you will have a better chance of establishing a foothold.

If you go head to head, as a player without a track record, without a reputation and possibly with fewer resources, you may find that you have to compete on price. This is a major factor in the high failure rate of businesses in the first couple of years after inception.

CHAPTER 6: BUSINESS DESCRIPTION

There is no existing business to describe, but convincing the reader that you have a clear vision of what it will be is vital. Investors are unlikely to be impressed by an idea for a business which has clearly not been thought through. The business planning process described in this book can help you think through your business idea and put meat on the bones. When you have completed the process you may well have radically changed what you intend to do.

It is a lot cheaper to discover that ideas are unworkable at the planning stage than to use trial and error in the field. Most plans change quite a lot on exposure to the marketplace anyway. The intention here is to eliminate the obvious.

Business name

Choosing a name is difficult. Try to make it memorable, not too difficult to pronounce and not cheesy. If the name describes what you do then fine, but finding a suitable one can be difficult.

Think about a distinctive logo. This is your company name or brand presented in a distinctive way which makes it more recognisable. Play with you computer fonts or talk to a graphic designer. When you have chosen a logo, use it on everything: business cards, letterheads, leaflets, adverts, van signs, etc. You will only pay for it once and then use it a lot so it may well be worth professionally designing it.

Legal

Most new businesses start life as *sole traderships*. This is someone trading as an individual and possibly employing people. The business is 100% owned by one person and the owner is personally liable for all its debts.

A *partnership* is similar but the ownership is spread between two or more individuals. Each of those owners are jointly liable for all the debts incurred, so be careful when choosing whom you go into partnership with. Everything you own is at risk.

A *limited company* is a legal entity in itself, has to be registered at Companies House and is subject to more complicated accounting procedures so your accountant's bill will be higher. You will be an employee of the company, not self-employed, so you may have to pay more tax. Apart from the investment you make in the business your personal assets are normally protected. Your bank manager may still insist that you personally guarantee a loan, however. If you want to give part of the business to investors, the organisation will have to be a limited company.

Location

State where you plan to trade from and what geographical area you plan to cover. Describe the premises, its size and the reasons for your choice. Many new businesses are started from home and, if practical, there is nothing wrong with that. The reduction in outlay and commitment can reduce the risk significantly. Check the deeds of your home first for restrictive covenants.

Achievements to date

You may think that as you haven't started you have no achievements. But think again. Have you developed a better mousetrap? Have you devised a more efficient way of operating? Have you discovered a hidden market?

If you have spent 200 hours on research and development the reader should be told about it. The effort you have made and the benefits of that effort are being invested in the business by you. Sadly, wasted hours going up dead ends count for nothing; but focus on what you have actually achieved.

CHAPTER 7: PRODUCTS AND SERVICES

Working on level 1 alone at this stage should suffice for most people.

All your products and services are new ones, so try not to have too many of them to start. Starting with a wide range does offer a bigger market to aim at, but does also result in a dilution of effort.

You probably do not have a surfeit of resources and should be wary of spreading them too thinly. Concentrating all your efforts on a narrow range of what you believe you can do best will allow you to make a bigger impact. You will also probably make fewer mistakes.

CHAPTER 8: CRITICAL SUCCESS FACTORS

This is very important in a start-up. Just work at level 1 and try to get an understanding of what *really* matters in this business.

Once you have determined what your CSFs are, try really hard to find a way in which you can do them better than your competitors. This really can be the difference between success and failure, so make sure you give it enough attention.

CHAPTER 9: SWOTTING YOUR COMPETITORS

Most people starting in business anew would definitely restrict themselves to level 1 at this stage.

The key difference with a start-up is that you cannot assess your performance because you haven't started yet, so you need a slightly different approach.

Strengths and weaknesses

First choose the ten things that matter most to the success of your business. Start with your CSFs (Chapter 8) and build from there. These are your *indicators*.

Decide who you think will be your three main competitors and assess them each out of 10 for their performance in each indicator. You may feel at this stage that you need to do more research on the competition and, if so, that's fine.

On the basis of the resources and experience you are putting into the business, hypothetically assess what your rating would be for each of the indicators.

You will now be able to create your SWOT. (Figure 19.1 gives a competitor analysis worksheet.)

Indicators	Competitor 1: name	Competitor 2: name	Competitor 3: name	Us
1. (describe)				
2. (describe)				
3. (describe)				
4. (describe)				
5. (describe)				
6. (describe)				
7. (describe)				
8. (describe)				
9. (describe)				
10. (describe)				

Figure 19.1   Competitor analysis worksheet

CHAPTER 10: DEVELOPING YOUR VISION

Level 1 is completely appropriate as it stands.

CHAPTER 11: BUSINESS STRATEGY

Again level 1 should suffice at start-up. Rather than looking at what should be changed, use all that you have learnt about the marketplace to develop your strategic position. This is how you are actually going to win in the battle with your competitors.

Investors are always looking for a strong strategy, as this is a big indication of the return they can expect to get. It is also a big indication of the return that *you* can expect to get from your business. So pay it very close attention!

If, after analysing the market and trying to develop your strategy, it just doesn't look as good as you thought it was going to be, don't be afraid to drop the whole thing and look for a better opportunity. Too many people have wasted too much money pursuing dreams without substance. When

179

you have done the research, it's not being negative to accept the inevitable. Large organisations often analyse many potential projects before actually embarking on one. *This one little tip can save you thousands.*

CHAPTER 12: OBJECTIVES

Use level 1 only. At start-up the focus will probably be on creating your external plan. It's still worth doing an internal plan as well because it will improve your chances of success. It is important to have objectives but don't regard them as being set in stone, because without any past performance to refer to it is difficult to work out what should be aimed at.

In the first year, review your performance against objectives at least monthly and where objectives are found to be unrealistic, adapt them and remodel your plan.

If, for example, it was found that the sales forecast was overly ambitious and needed to be scaled back by 10%, then that would have repercussions throughout the business. It could mean a projected first year's profit turning into a loss. This may necessitate finding economies to avoid running out of money.

It is far easier to make the changes at this stage rather than when the money has gone. This is a key advantage of planning and reviewing regularly.

TOP TIP

The importance of having goals and modifying them in light of experience cannot be overemphasised, because without them you tend to drift.

CHAPTER 13: YOUR MARKETING PLAN

It is more difficult to estimate what sales and costs will be when there is no past performance to refer to. None the less, establishing a budget is essential because without it you have no way of knowing how much money you will actually need.

This is where all the research you have carried out will come in very handy. Fill in the forms as best you can, using all the information you have, but bear in mind that no amount of research compares with actually getting out there and doing it. As stated previously, *once you have some actual trading figures* you will need to review your plan regularly and, if necessary, adapt it.

CHAPTER 14: OPERATIONS PLAN

This is the part of the plan where you have the opportunity to convince the reader that you have the capability to deliver.

With an existing business this section explains how the business operates, while here you are saying how you plan to do it.

Running through this section is a great way of crystallising your thinking. It forces you to say exactly *how* things will be done. Don't overdo the detail, however; you are not trying to give someone a recipe for starting the business themselves!

Make sure that the capacity you are planning matches the sales figure in your marketing plan.

CHAPTER 15: MANAGEMENT

Outline the skills of the people you already have and those you will be acquiring from people you plan to recruit. Thinking this through is very important because the lack of an experienced team who have worked together successfully for some time is generally a primary weakness of a new business. You need to demonstrate that you plan to assemble a team methodically with all the required skills.

It is perfectly acceptable for businesses to get skills from professional advisers as well as employees. Make good use of your accountant and trusted consultants. They can provide expertise that would be very expensive in a full-time employee. Demonstrate to the reader that you have thought of everything and covered all bases as well as could be expected.

CHAPTER 16: FINANCE

This is where many people fall down when they are trying to raise money to launch their first business.

If you have submitted your plan to an investor and get invited to a meeting, your understanding of the numbers will probably be severely tested. If you have simply passed this part to your accountant to do, or just put in numbers you cannot justify, you could easily become unstuck in the meeting.

Make sure you understand the numbers – they must reflect what the rest of the plan has said, and they must make sense.

Clearly the sales figures have to match up with the marketing plan; costs have to match the production plan, etc.

Sometimes it is only when the financial plan is completed that one discovers a business to be not viable. There is no shame in abandoning a business idea at this stage to find a better opportunity. Sometimes an investor who is far more experienced at evaluating business ideas than you are will see something in the figures that you missed.

If an investor turns the proposal down get feedback as to why. Some ideas just will not fly and, if that is really the case, the sooner one moves on to something better, the better.

CHAPTER 17: GETTING RESULTS

This chapter applies equally to a new business but comes after the money has actually been raised. The problem with raising money, of course, is that once you have it, you need to deliver. This part helps you turn investment to profit.

Good luck.

Further Reading

CHAPTER 4: MARKET

Philip Kotler, *Principles of Marketing*, Prentice Hall, 2010.

CHAPTER 7: PRODUCTS AND SERVICES

Malcolm McDonald, *Marketing Plans*, Elsevier, 2005 (product audit section).

CHAPTER 8: CSF

Malcolm McDonald, *Marketing Plans*, Elsevier, 2005 (customer and market audit section).

CHAPTER 10: VISION

Jim Collins and Jerry Porras, *Built to last*, Random House, 2005.
Jack Welch, *Winning*, HarperCollins, 2005.

CHAPTER 11: STRATEGY

Michael Porter, *Competitive Strategy*, Free Press, 2004.
Chan Kim and Renee Mouborgne, *Blue Ocean Strategy*, Harvard Business School Press, 2005.
Henry Mintzberg, *The Rise and Fall of Strategic Planning*, Prentice Hall, 2000.

CHAPTER 13: MARKETING PLAN

Malcolm McDonald, *Marketing Plans*, Elsevier, 2005.

CHAPTER 14: OPERATIONS PLAN

Richard Ling and Walter Goddard, *Orchestrating Success*, John Wiley, 1992.

CHAPTER 15: MANAGEMENT

Michael Armstrong, *Handbook of HRM*, Kogan Page, 2009.

CHAPTER 16: FINANCE

Gene Sicilanico, *Finance for Non-financial Managers*, McGraw Hill, 2003.

CHAPTER 18: GAINING ACCEPTANCE

Nicholas Oulton, *Killer Presentations*, How To Books, 2007.

Index